D1306567

THE KEEPERS

John F. Blair, Publisher

Winston-Salem, North Carolina

The Keepers

MOUNTAIN FOLK

HOLDING ON TO

OLD SKILLS

AND TALENTS

NARRATIVE BY ROBERT ISBELL
PHOTOGRAPHS BY ARTHUR TILLEY

DESIGN BY DEBRA LONG HAMPTON

PRINTED AND BOUND IN CANADA BY TRANSCONTINENTAL PRINTING

*The paper in this book meets the guidelines for permanence
and durability of the Committee on Production Guidelines
for Book Longevity of the Council on Library Resources.*

Library of Congress Cataloging-in-Publication Data

    The keepers : mountain folk holding on to old skills and talents / text
by Robert Isbell ; photographs by Arthur Tilley.

        p.   cm.

    Includes index.

    ISBN 0-89587-180-7 (alk. paper)

    1. Folk art—Appalachian Region, Southern.   2. Arts—Appalachian
Region, Southern. I. Tilley, Arthur. II. Title.

NX506.I82   1999

700'.92'27568—dc21   99–17456

CONTENTS

ACKNOWLEDGMENTS

There were cordial, helpful, often scholarly people who wanted to see this book published. They made the task pleasant, and we are grateful.

A few of them may be surprised to see their names here, yet in some way they contributed:

Steve Kirk, of Winston-Salem, for his talented work as editor and for his vigilance against lapses

Sally Hill McMillan, of Charlotte, for her quick response as a literary agent and for her knowledge of the market

Carolyn Sakowski, of Winston-Salem, for her confidence in publishing this book

Debbie Hampton, of Winston-Salem, for her excellence of design

Meredith Bozek, of Miami, for her interest, generosity, talent, and advice

The staffs of the Watauga County Library and the Ashe County Chamber of Commerce, for directing us to interesting people in these pages

For their many kindnesses: Peggy Glenn Campbell, Donna and Gene Chaires, Jane and John Champion, Frankie and Jim Childress, Rowena Collier, Camilla and Robert Dick, Sarah and Dick Dillon, Aysel and Fred Dyer, Marbeth and Carl Fidler, Ellen and George Gray, Fran Isbell, Sarah and Oren Jones, Anand Karnad, Jan Karon, Laverne Kiser, Gloria Gaines Klugh, Marjon, Ann and Clyde Murchison, David Perry, Max Pritchard, Joe Shannon, Nell Mayer Taylor, Jim Thompson, Leslie Tilley, Ginny and John Tinnell, Jerry Torchia, Donna and Jack Upchurch, Barbara and Yardy Williams, and Margaret Woody

INTRODUCTION

The arts and crafts of pioneer people are performed almost solely in imitation today. Finely educated people create handmade items, sing primitive songs, and play stringed instruments. They perform well—often better than their predecessors—but rarely does their product come from related folk origins.

Yet, incredibly, authentic skills of bygone days still exist. Hidden in the coves and valleys of the Appalachians are diminishing numbers of artists and artisans who still conform to the teachings of their forebears. They practice crafts and sing and dance in ways handed down for more than two centuries—from mothers and fathers to daughters and sons.

The Keepers deals with a cross-section of such people. It lays open a continuum of ancient skills that, combined with stories of mountain life, allows an outsider to peek into prior times.

Oh God! put back Thy universe
and give me yesterday.

Henry Herman (1832–94)

Herb Gatherer

TED HICKS

TED HICKS WAS BORN in an unpainted two-story house on a fifty-seven-acre cabbage and potato farm. The farthest he has ever strayed from this home "under the Beech" was to Spartanburg, not three hours away and just south of the North Carolina line. For the most part his world extends no farther than he can see from the mountaintop. On clear nights on the peak above his home he can look beyond the easternmost ridges of Tennessee to the distal, flickering lights of Elizabethton, Johnson City, and Bristol. These are the only other far places he has ever been.

He is aware but uncaring of his anomaly in a high-flown era in which people either follow a groove or glory in rebellion. He knows that each side falls into prevailing norms; he begrudges neither; he does not covet or fear; he does not flaunt his distinction or give it much thought. To him life is good; his place in the world is proper.

"I've never gone what you call far," he says. "I ain't got out of the rolling land yet."

"And that makes no difference to you?"

"No. Could have gone far out, but never saw much need to."

"But millions out there are wealthy, even famous. If you could be one of them, who would it be?"

"I reckon it'd still be me."

"What work would you choose?"

"I'd gather herbs. Just like what I do now. It's what I like to do. Like to pull galax. Like being out in the woods. Like hunting, getting out. Peaceful like. Mostly up on the mountain [Beech], but I go other places, too. Go to Rich Mountain, look for 'sang [ginseng] there. But it's beginning to lose its wildness. Houses being built there like at the Beech. Changed in the last ten years. Used to [be] you might meet maybe only one car over there; anymore you meet several

of them. Civilization keeps on coming, which helps out, makes a lot of jobs and stuff, but you lose the other things. I always did like it in the woods, but it's getting harder to get away from things, especially around where I've been at. I guess there's still a lot of places where, you know, it's natural—like probably out west, or Alaska, something like that."

On a bright morning in May the sun spreads over the steep mountainside. Cool winds gusting down from Virginia scour clouds in an otherwise empty sky. Trees, shrubs, and wildflowers bob and sway. It is an in-between

Ted Hicks,
Beech Mountain, North Carolina

season for gathering herbs and plants, but Ted wants to assay the potential harvest; he leads the way to the lush thickets above his home.

"Now this is mayapple," he says as he fingers new spring leaves. "Here, see the flower underneath. Blooms this month. That's why we call it mayapple. Some say it's mandrake, like in the Bible, but we call it mayapple. Smells good; smells like a banana. You can eat it. Tastes like a banana, too. It'll be ready in the fall. Best to dig the roots then. But it's not been on 'the list' in the last two or three years. Plenty of it, though."

Drug manufacturers use the mayapple's plump underground stems in the preparation of purgatives. Ted thinks the remedy has been in use "since the days of Indians."

"The list" refers to a sheet issued by Wilcox, an old company in Boone where Ted sells his gathered medicinal herbs and plants. Each season Wilcox's management provides a list of items needed. This year mayapple is not among the herbs it seeks.

"But now witch hazel leaf—beadwood we call it—they're buying that, and I can get plenty. Don't have to go much outside our place here to get lots of it."

Ted harvests beadwood in the fall. He sells its dried leaves and sometimes its bark. Drug companies use it to produce liniments.

On a cool morning several Octobers ago Ted was off to himself pulling beadwood leaves at the edge of a forest. Through the thick underbrush he could hear the rustle of leaves as his father, his brother Leonard, and his young cousin Michael from Tennessee worked together. To ward off the chill the men wore denim jackets; the boy wore a red coat.

Ted had nearly filled his sack with leaves when he heard a strange noise beyond the towering shrubs.

M-m-m, m-m, uh, m-m, went the sound.

"I looked back there toward the noise, holding the sack, you know, and the bushes just—*whoosh*—fell apart."

A dark form sprang through the foliage, and Ted threw down his sack and ran toward a locust tree. Trying desperately to get out of range of the great beast, he had neither the time nor the inclination to identify it. To him, at the moment, it was just black, huge, and attacking. As he ran he yelled to his companions and, in passing, frantically tore a large branch from the tree—"something to fight with, you know."

On came the critter, crashing through Ted's sack and scattering beadwood leaves over the forest floor. By then Ted had reached the other leaf gatherers and was yelling, particularly to his cousin.

"I didn't want Michael hurt atter he'd come from Tennessee to see us—my mother's brother's son. I hollered for him to get up a tree. He said, 'I can't climb,' and they told me later that I was a-trying to push him up the tree. The black thing—I figured it was a bear—rounded the bushes and was a-coming at us. Now I could see it, could make out what it was. It was a bull. A big, black Angus bull. And my cousin a-wearing that red coat.

"Well, my brother was already trying to cut off a limb with his pocketknife, but he didn't have enough time, so he grabbed three or four rocks and started throwing at the bull, and it kept a-coming. I was waving my locust limb a-trying to keep it away from my cousin, and then I looked up. There Michael was in the top of the tree. Him in that red coat. Couldn't climb, you know.

"Leonard threw one rock and missed; he threw another, and it just shaved the bull's nose. But that caused him to turn left and tear out of there. Just a rock, you know. Barely hit it.

"Well, we grabbed up the beadwood and got out of there before he took it in his head to come back."

He cannot remember—he estimates he was "maybe five or six"—when his father began taking him up on the mountain to gather herbs and plants. "I could barely get through the woods, but herbing got in my blood. I'd dig and carry things for Dad. Could do galax

pretty good, too."

The father, Ray Hicks, is said to be the country's premier teller of Jack Tales, but his storytelling income alone was never enough to keep the family going. Therefore, besides farming potatoes and cabbage, Ray Hicks supplemented his income by gathering bounty from the forests.

"That's what they did in my family long before I can remember," says Ted. "We gathered herbs and things. My great-great-granddaddy—Samuel was his name—was the first to enter this country. Homesteaded right over yander—can't see from here—and paid for that old rocky land by selling herbs. Couldn't have made it without herbs."

So little Ted Hicks followed a line of herb gatherers—from Samuel to son Benjamin, to Benjamin's son Nathan, and then to Ray and Ray's children. But Ted thinks he may be the last of the herb gatherers in his family. He remains unmarried. He grins as he shakes his head and "guesses" he has waited too late. "Just have to look now," he says. He believes that, for all his decades of combing the woods, his father still knows more about the herbs and plants.

"I learned from him. Learned how to find the plants, to pull them in the right season, to dry them, and to sell them."

It was not long after his first trips with his father that he began to go "herbing" with his brother Leonard, five years his senior, who also learned herb gathering from the father. Leonard would pull witch hazel, and Ted would hold the bag. Later, when sickness began to curtail father Ray's trips into the forests, Leonard and Ted took up the slack.

"It kept us in clothes," says Ted. "Enough for school."

In those days herbs were the main source for medicines, but in the decades since, synthetics have come along and cut demand. Ted remembers the herb market was once so active that the drug company would send a truck around to pick up the harvests.

"Me'n Leonard, we'd stack witch hazel leaves up there at the house and be waiting for the truck to come. They'd be there at a certain time, and they'd have scales—to weigh the herbs, you know. Pay us right there."

"Me'n Leonard. They said where you'd see one you'd see the other. We all got along pretty good. Leonard was the oldest; then a sister two years younger. I'm the middle one. Then there's two other sisters. All of them live over the line in Tennessee, and Leonard still comes over and we go galax pulling. He comes over nearly every Saturday. The girls come up every once in a while.

"We got along good, all of us, except maybe there'd be pillow fights, even hair pulling, but we were pretty close. When it was too cold to get out we'd play chess. Had a little chessboard; learned the moves from the directions; learned that the castle goes straight on both sides, that the horse jumps around, but the king could go just one space at the time. The king, we thought, ought to be boss, go anywhere he wanted to.

"We played other games, too—Monopoly—and we listened to Dad tell stories. That was in winter. But even then, when the weather was right, me'n Leonard would go out and pull galax or wild cherry bark. Beadwood bark, too. Just have to hew beadwood off in the winter. See, when there's sap in it, it'll strip good, but in winter there ain't no sap. You just have to hew the bark off. We'd bring beadwood into the house and cut it, burn the wood that's left. Smells good when it's burning. Fume up your house."

Also during the coldest months, Ted and Leonard hunted rabbits and grouse to supplement the family diet. There would be corn and beans that mother Rosa canned in late summer and stored for the winter in a little house they called the cellar, above the spring.

"Hardly ever freezes there," says Ted. "We'd line the potato box with pasteboard. Makes good insulation. It'd have to stay real cold for a week or so before it freezes anything. We had only a few potatoes to freeze on us.

"Now, cabbage. Seems like cabbages draw the cold in. They'll freeze pretty hard, but when they thaw out they're just as good as ever. In the winter we'd just pull them up from the ground, roots and all, and leave the roots sticking up. Dig a trench and cover them with dirt upside down. Somebody came there once and said, 'Gollay, I didn't know cabbage growed that way.' "

From January through March the weather was rarely inviting for those who lived in the high mountains. For days that seemed like months frigid weather kept Ted and Leonard out of their beloved forests; they yearned to walk in the woods; they needed to "limber up" their bodies, to shake off the torpid effects of being so long confined to the parlor, sitting close to an ancient stove.

There were days when the wind was calm and only a dusting of snow lay upon the forest floor. At such times Ted and Leonard were out after daybreak. Despite the forbidding season there were treasures to be found.

"See, we could get out sometimes, even in January. On pretty days we might get log moss. Sometimes, when the moss was wet, we'd have to hang it out in the woods, let it dry before we could carry it out. Wet log moss is awful heavy.

"That's off a dead log, you know, and it grows back after you peel it. That's why we always left just a little sprig. Then it gets the rain, and in a few years moss'll cover the log again. See, the log rots, and once it's all gone there's nothing for the moss to grow on, and it dies."

When log moss was dry enough the brothers would carry it from the woods in a bundle. "We'd always take twine and tie up the moss in a bale. Tie it tight, put it on our shoulders, and take it through the bushes. Take it down to the truck and go back for more."

After loading their truck the brothers would drive down to Pineola, about an hour away. There they sold the load to a company that prepared and marketed log moss for funeral carpets. Other uses were as decorations, as linings for hanging flowerpots, and as a substitute for peat moss.

On good days they would pick galax leaves, which will keep for many months in water. Wholesalers sell galax to florists, who use the green-to-bronze plant in flower arrangements.

Also in good weather, Ted and Leonard peeled wild black cherry bark. The product's end use was chiefly for treating coughs, bronchitis, and colds.

Ted likes to peel wild cherry bark in the winter, because there is then little danger of livestock eating the wilting leaves. "When wild cherry begins to shrink," he says, "and when a horse or cow comes up and eats it, it sort of packs their stomach and kills them. I've known about several cows killed like that. See, if you cut a wild cherry and there's a cow around, you better carry the brush off and burn it." In the winter, he explains, the leaves are dead, most of them blown away or decaying into the soil, past the poisonous stage.

Even as a boy Ted learned to conserve the precious plants he harvested. His father taught him early to leave sprigs so the log moss could regenerate and to cut down the wild cherry trees at their base, because if they were stripped without cutting they would die eventually.

"But the little roots you leave, so the sprouts can grow from them. I've seen fifteen, maybe twenty sprouts come up where you cut it. Can't take off that bark around where the young sprouts come up. Leave the roots and little trees come back, like a locust does."

Ted thinks the flagrant abuse of the forests began with the early settlers and continues today. He cites the rape of ginseng, perhaps the most popular medicinal herb ever gathered: " 'Sang comes in September. That's when the berries are red. I just throw back the berries so the plant will come back; it takes about seven years for it to be fully grown. But too many people just take the whole plant. In a hurry, you know. So much

of that has killed a lot of beds."

For centuries the Chinese attributed mystical powers to the ginseng plant. Today some think the shape of the straight, two-pronged root is why ginseng is used as an aphrodisiac. "The 'sang roots can look like a little man," says Ted. "Got two legs, sometimes two arms, and a 'quirl' that looks like a head."

The Chinese importation of American ginseng is the direct cause of its alarming decline in the Appalachians, where it once grew in abundance. The beds remaining, Ted thinks, will one day be no more. He says the laws now governing the harvesting of ginseng will not be enough; there is too little concern for the plants' regeneration, too much building on lands where ginseng grows.

Ted's father, Ray, ruefully recalls the killing of the plants' beds: "Back then, when Ted was a boy, there was ginseng above Whaley, way up on that wing yander, what they called Buckeye Creek. All that in there was in 'sang. There's still some there, but they won't let you gather it now—where they've got their homes, all that golf course. Yiah, when they built the homes up on the Beech, they pushed out big patches. Didn't know they was doing it, you know.

"The last I gathered—it was with my uncle and Ted—was in the Rich Mountain above Boone. And people are living in there now, a-killing all that 'sang. Well, I always sowed the seeds back. Honest people do that, bury the seeds up in the leaves. Lot of people bring out the seeds with the berries. I'd leave mine. With a feeling, you know. Just have to do that with your feelings."

Though he lived distant from his contemporaries Ted Hicks does not remember loneliness. Besides the companionship of brother Leonard, Ted often roamed the woods with his best friend and cousin, Orville Hicks. At times Orville would bring friends.

"You'd see them a-coming on their bicycles, maybe four or five of them. They'd come and would tell jokes. We hunted rabbits and grouse, but mostly we just walked in the woods."

Ted and Orville could identify the trees and shrubs and animals of the mountain forests.

"We didn't care about the Latin names," he says. "We knew the trees and shrubs by the names we were told to call them—oaks, pines, chestnuts, walnuts, sarvices [serviceberry], buckeyes, beech, sourwoods, laurel, and ivy.

"One time the science teacher at Valle Crucis took the class into the forest, up on the Beech, and he'd stop and say, 'Who knows the name of this tree?' If nobody'd answer he'd ask me, because he knew I spent so much time in the woods. Then, when we'd tell him

the name of the tree, the one we knew, he'd tell us the scientific name. But one time he asked the name of a tree that the others didn't know. I'd drifted behind everybody, you know, so he hollered, 'Where's Ted?' Well, I came up and saw the tree. Couldn't tell what it was. Then I looked on the ground, and there was a walnut in the leaves, and I said, 'Black walnut tree!' Nobody knew that I'd been stumped; all that saved me was that walnut a-lying on the ground."

No matter the season, Ted and Orville ranged the woods. They knew the ways of the animals—foxes, groundhogs, rabbits, raccoons, possums, red squirrels, and chipmunks. They studied the birds—wrens, finches, cardinals, chewinks (towhees), snowbirds (juncos), and mockingbirds; on rare occasions they might see a scarlet tanager or a rose-breasted grosbeak.

Sometimes Ted visited Orville, who was born and reared in a place called Sandy Flat.

"Orville's dad was a preacher. Pretty strict. And Orville didn't have funny books. So me'n Leonard, we'd sneak them to him. Orville told me once that when he seen my dad a-coming he knew me'n Leonard would be with him, knew we'd be bringing funny books. We didn't even let my dad know about the funny books. Dad probably wouldn't mind, but we sort of figured it best to keep funny books hid."

Even today cousin Orville—though busy

with his obligations—remains a close friend. He spends a few Saturday afternoons with Ted in the forests; still, family life causes him to visit less often.

"Sometimes he'll come over," says Ted. "We'll pitch horseshoes, just like long time ago."

Ted's father, in his seventies, is not able to get around as he once did. He often must refuse invitations to recite folk tales; apparently even his annual trips to the storytelling festival in Jonesborough, Tennessee, are numbered. When people ask if Ted will succeed him Ray shakes his head: "Ted knows the stories, but he ain't going to follow me; he can't stand that many people."

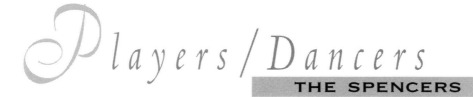

Players/Dancers

THE SPENCERS

As a boy, living beneath the peaks of Virginia's tallest mountains, a thing happened to nine-year-old Albert Hash that would direct his life.

He was hoeing in a cornfield one afternoon when lightning struck close by. Instantly thunder came and then a downpour. Sudden storms are common in the mountain summers, and an uncle, Corbett Stamper, was happy to take in the drenched and breathless Albert, who came pounding at his door.

As the boy waited out the storm he grew fascinated by the fine wood and elegant curves of his uncle's fiddle on the wall. Stamper rarely permitted others to hold the instrument, but perceiving the boy's interest he took down the fiddle and began playing. It was, Albert said later, the prettiest sound he ever heard. Stamper yielded to the boy's enchantment and laid the instrument in his hands. Albert carefully inspected it; he was smitten; he wanted such an instrument and considered how he might have one, learn to play one.

In the months after, Albert could not get his uncle's fiddle off his mind. He priced violins in mail-order catalogs but knew that there was no way for a ten-year-old boy to make enough money to buy one. Then one night he had a dream in which he constructed a fiddle. When he arose in the morning he found an ammunition crate. With a pencil he drew a pattern of

Martha, Emily, Thornton, and Kilby Spencer, Mouth of Wilson, Virginia

the fiddle he remembered on his uncle's wall. With his father's handsaw he cut out crude pieces smaller than those of his uncle's violin, the size dictated by the width and length of the crate. He tacked the front, back, and sides together; he did not know how to glue fiddle pieces. The result was a fiddle of sorts, enough to please him.

He had not thought to examine the bow of his uncle's fiddle. From a willow stick he whittled a bow roughly as he remembered it. To obtain hair for it, he and his brother hemmed a horse in a fence corner, but when he tried to pull the hair from the horse's tail the animal bucked. "It nearly jerked my arm off," Albert later said. He thought it a piece of luck that a neighbor tipped him a quarter to go to a country store for supplies. At the store Albert saw a fiddle string; the price was exactly a quarter.

Now he had constructed a bow and a fiddle, but when he pulled the bow across the strings there was no sound. It was a neighbor boy who came to the rescue. He had once learned to play simple fiddle tunes, and he knew the problem. "You ain't got no rosin," said the boy. "I'll go home and get you some rosin."

When the neighbor boy returned he stroked rosin upon the strings. Then, taking

Albert's fiddle in hand, he reclined on the ground, laid his head on a chopping block, and tucked the crude fiddle under his chin. He played roughly and awkwardly; the boys smiled happily; they were delighted that the homemade instrument produced recognizable sounds at all.

As his friend played, Albert watched. Later he took his fiddle into the house and sat behind the cookstove. Over and over he attempted the simple songs the neighbor boy played. To his disappointment he could produce only screeches and scratches.

Mercifully, perhaps, his brother accidentally sat upon and smashed the homemade fiddle. Their father, aware of Albert's drive to have his own instrument, finally ordered one from Montgomery Ward. With the new fiddle, Albert learned to play—learned well enough to know that a mail-order fiddle could not satisfy him. Eventually he obtained drawings for the kind of fiddle professional musicians played; he constructed a fiddle of his own, cutting it from premium materials, searching for a better tone. It was Corbett Stamper, the man who had brought Albert in from the storm, who taught the boy to refine his fiddling. From that point forward Albert Hash's love of fiddles never left him.

Albert married a comely young woman who lived in the remote Fees Branch area, near the North Carolina border. Her brother, Thornton Spencer, was seven at the time. Within two years Thornton was spending much of his time at the Hash home, admiring his brother-in-law's mastery of the violin. (There's a saying in the Virginia mountains: "A violin is just a fiddle that's been to college.") It was Albert who taught the young Thornton to play.

Albert's making and playing of fiddles and dulcimers influenced the preservation of old-time music in southwestern Virginia. He not only prolonged a heritage of mountain music, he actually brought about a revival. There are festivals and contests year-round in the mountain areas, and Albert Hash disciples are prominent. In Ashe County, North Carolina, there is an annual Albert Hash Festival, and students of Mount Rogers School in Virginia have an Albert Hash Memorial Band. He is honored in the Grayson Highlands State Park visitor center. There his likeness is on murals, and his exquisitely carved violin is displayed in a glass case.

Albert died in 1983, and he lies in a graveyard by a meadow on the slope of Haw Orchard Mountain, not two hundred yards from the dwelling of his most ardent follower, Thornton Spencer. Thornton and his wife, Emily, carry on. They teach mountain music, and they play somewhere every week: Wolftrap, Sparta, Fries, Glendale Springs, Clarksboro, Raccoon Holler, Union Grove, Laurel Springs, Stuart, Floyd, Mount Airy, the Barter Theater at Abingdon—places throughout Virginia, Tennessee, North Carolina, West Virginia, Kentucky, and Ohio.

Thornton and Emily sustain the love of pioneer music handed down by Albert Hash. Now their children—Kilby, fourteen, and Martha, eleven—are the legatees. Thornton plays the fiddle and guitar; Emily, the banjo, guitar, and fiddle; Kilby, the guitar and bass fiddle; and Martha, the guitar and banjo. On weekends the Spencers pack their paraphernalia and travel to some music-and-dance event. Thornton and Emily play with the Whitetop Mountain Band, and Kilby and Martha dance—flatfoot, waltz, square dance, Virginia reel.

Years ago it was at a mountain-music event that a friend introduced Thornton to a young woman from Arlington, Virginia, a recent graduate of Clinch Valley College. The woman, Emily Paxton, had come to hear regionally prominent banjoist Stuart Carrico of Pine Mountain. Thornton was there to play along with Carrico.

Clearly Emily was not a mountain woman, but she had always wanted to live in the mountains; she happily chose to join Thornton and come into the quiet milieu of his life. There she embraced his musical friends and helped carve out a modest live-lihood by playing, singing, and teaching music handed down from Thornton's pioneer ancestors. To supplement their income they worked at farming.

Now, with their two children, they live hidden from the highway in a small home at the dead end of a rugged, one-way lane. Antique furnishings—gifts of Emily's mother—share rooms already crowded with musical instruments. It is a happy house, and music and dancing prevail.

"We're alone here," says Emily. "A few come to music lessons, but there are never strangers unless somebody is hopelessly lost." She says the summers are pleasant and the winters severe. "The wind from Mount Rogers is fierce. It leaves there and comes right down through us. People tell us they bet the wind doesn't hit us in this holler, but it'll knock you down sometimes."

To Kilby and his sister, growing up in a musical family is play. The two are at ease with instruments and are obsessed with dancing.

When he was younger Kilby was a precocious dancer, but for a few years he lost interest. Now, when the band strikes up, he and Martha are invariably the first to take the floor.

Martha has taken no hiatus from dancing. She danced before she could walk alone; in her walker her tiny feet kept time whenever she heard the beat of music. Later, as a toddler, Martha would watch intently as her sitter, a sister of Thornton's, danced to canned music. Martha would observe her aunt's motions, and soon the two were dancing flatfoot to the tunes her parents played on the radio.

Thornton says that Kilby and Martha come by their dancing naturally, because music making and dancing have always been in his family. When Eleanor Roosevelt came to Appalachia in 1936 she presented prizes at a Whitetop Mountain festival. It was Thornton's grandfather who, with his buck-and-wing steps, won the dancing award.

Thornton and Emily are sensitive to their self-imposed challenge to preserve mountain music, but they think that playing and dancing must be enjoyed, must never be a task. They tell of how Martha, only three at the time, became fascinated by a woman who jumped high off the floor when she danced. On the way home Martha told her parents that the woman couldn't dance, though she thought the woman "had an awful big time."

"We've never pushed Kilby and Martha," Thornton says. "If they wanted to dance, okay; if they didn't, okay. I'm sure that if we'd have pushed them they'd be better, but kids don't really want lessons. They'll learn good for a while, but when they get bigger they burn out. It's fun for Martha and Kilby.

They've never worked at it. Hard work takes the fun out of it for kids."

Thornton thinks neither child will want to make a living out of playing and dancing. He says that for them it's just something that's part of life.

The main street of Sparta, North Carolina, runs roughly east-west near the top of a ridge, where stately homes still stand amid the business district. Sparta has long been a center of cattle raising; it is the place where Dr. Grabow presmoked pipes are made; it was the home of the late "Farmer Bob" Doughton, once the senior member of Congress and a founder of the Blue Ridge Parkway.

On the sidewalk outside the Alleghany Jubilee Hall, Friday-night dancers gather early, some in plain street dress, others in store-bought Western garb, and still others in costumes created in sewing rooms and on kitchen tables. They come from seventy miles around. By eight o'clock they have filed into the old theater and seated themselves along the walls on both sides of the plywood-covered dance floor. American flags are draped behind them. At the south end of the floor members of the Whitetop Mountain Band tune their instruments, a tedious exercise. In their last appearance, says one band member, the group was out of tune the whole night.

When at last the cacophony ends the dance caller steps to the microphone. He chides those sitting along the sides and back of the old theater: "Now tonight I want everybody out here dancing. Don't be bashful; don't just watch. Get out there and join this first dance. A flatfoot dance. Nobody's too old or too young. The first tune the Whitetop Mountain boys and girls will play is 'Ebenezer.' "

There are four musicians tonight; one of the two guitarists could not come. Thornton is the fiddler and Emily the banjoist. Playing with them are a guitarist and a bass fiddler. Martha, who has been chatting with the dancers along the wall—a few of them seven times her age—cannot keep still. Her feet tick rhythmically upon the plywood, the steel taps making soft, metallic sounds as she sways gently to a beat that others cannot hear. Kilby stands in the middle of the floor laughing with young friends. At this point no one else has come out to dance. As if by signal Martha and Kilby take young partners and stand poised. The band now strikes up, and the young ones are joined by a few couples. As the lively "Ebenezer" swells, others steal upon the scene, and suddenly the chairs along the walls are vacant as a hundred dancers spill onto the pad. The floor is packed, but the couples do not mind; a feverish bond conjoins hoofers and musicians.

Like Lippizaner stallions, the dancers fall into a prance. Their movements are a two-step variant of the very old flatfoot dance, itself a derivative of the buck dance and the Irish jig. As their steel taps thunder their bodies pulsate to the throb of "Ebenezer," and they do not smile. They are at the same time disco hoofers and old-time cloggers. Squaring off, they pump arms and legs powerfully, locomotive pistons thrusting to the band's cadence. They dance straight on, but they look past their partners to the flags on the wall, to the ceiling, to their drumming feet. It is as though they are dangled from strings like fitful marionettes.

The frenzied pace goes on for fifteen, twenty minutes before "Ebenezer" comes to an end. The dancers shuffle to the sidelines briefly to rest. Tireless Martha remains at the edge of the dance pad; she taps about and banters with adult friends.

Minutes later the caller announces that the next dance will be a waltz. This time there is no delay; participants quickly fill the floor and begin what one might expect to be an eighteenth-century waltz. But it is not to be. Though the band plays three-quarter time, waltz steps are barely evident. It is a hybrid dance. The tapping feet and other innovations of the hills give a robustness and heavy beat to the gliding waltz of old. Now the dancers touch; they hold each other stiffly as in a common waltz, but their moves are worlds away from the old formal ballrooms.

Next comes a square dance little different from square dances of any age, except that here there is not so much foot shuffling as foot tapping.

At the first intermission Emily mingles easily among the participants. Thornton sits on the stage and studiously attends his violin. Emily says there is a balance tonight among the old, the middle-aged, and the young. She expects teenagers to begin coming in after the Sparta High football game ends.

The next set of dances is similar to the first, except that Emily sings on two occasions. She belts out the first song, but the second is soft and plaintive. The dancers hold their partners lightly and move at the three-quarter beat in which Emily sings a lilting "My Home Is in Whitetop Mountain." It has the flavor of old chanteys like "Shenandoah"; it is obviously of local origin but has a classic feel:

My old home's in Whitetop Mountain,
But I left and I went away,
And I often think of that old homeplace
Where I spent those happiest days.

When it's springtime in that mountain
And the moon is shining bright,
I'll be back in Whitetop Mountain
And I'll settle down for life.

One day I left that Whitetop Mountain
For old Mexico to roam,
And I traveled the West all over,
But I found no place like home.

When it's springtime in that mountain
And the moon is shining bright,
I'll be back in Whitetop Mountain
And I'll settle down for life.

And then my mind in the West did ramble
For me back east to go,
Back to that old Whitetop Mountain
And the loved ones that I used to know.

When it's springtime in that mountain
And the moon is shining bright,
I'll be back in Whitetop Mountain
And I'll settle down for life.

When the number ends someone points toward the rear of the audience to a ramrod-straight man in his eighties. He is Gene Carpenter, the song's composer. He says he "made up" the words and music just three years before; it's one of many songs he creates and carries in his head.

When the set ends Emily makes a beeline to the composer. He compliments her singing. They chat amiably. He is a native of Whitetop Mountain, but as a young man he went into the coal mines of West Virginia and worked underground, until black lung forced him to retire. He speaks with the resonance of a Carl Sandburg; his stories of folk heroes John Henry and John Hardy are remindful of the Klondike poet Robert Service. Carpenter's recollections, whether reflected or experienced, are bareknuckled and roughly sentimental. Though his folk tales come from coal-mine country they are of the ilk of sourdough and gold dust.

Martha, still flitting about and chatting to the delight of her elders, comes over to point out a man wearing a blue cap and blue shirt. "He's the dancer I've always watched," she whispers. "Him and his partner—awfully good."

It was after Martha had learned the buck dance that she often observed the man who this night, despite his skills, is modest and withdrawn. He has driven sixty-five miles to dance. He thinks Martha is a good mark, one who need not be told twice how to do a thing. She is one to observe and imitate until she masters her act. Once at Mabry Mill, off the Blue Ridge Parkway, Martha saw the "bear dance" performed. She came home and perfected a variation, the "possum dance," with which she soon delighted audiences. Face up, she dances on all fours in the fashion of Russian Cossacks.

To an outsider it is apparent that television and movies have altered the pioneer dances; there seems to be a bit of the Texas two-step in both flatfooting and the waltz. But Thornton and Emily Spencer take issue. "It's not the local people who are copying; it's the other way around." Thornton is positive: "I remember the two-step, like this one, being done by my granddaddy, and he got it from his granddaddy. The Texas two-step? He never heard of it."

Young Kilby is first on the floor after the second intermission. He carries a broom, its straw bent from the handle at a severe angle. Soon partners are chosen, and they take the floor, all but Kilby, who begins dancing with the broom. The dance is similar to the previous waltz, and the participants seem not to notice that Kilby dances without a human partner. He is hidden in the crowd when there comes a loud report. Quickly the male dancers leave their partners and scurry about grabbing new companions, and now Kilby can be seen dancing with a brightly dressed woman. Then out of the crowd a man emerges. Too slow to catch a partner, he suffers the penalty and now carries Kilby's broom. In a half-minute or so he drops the sweeping end to the floor and places his foot upon it. Holding the shaft's end to create tension, he suddenly releases the handle, and it slaps sharply upon the floor. Again the men leave their partners and scramble for new ones. The dance is a variation of an old children's game.

Although Albert Hash learned to play from his uncle Corbett, it was his own intensity and innovation that recharged interest in music and dancing. Up off Cabin Creek, where he lived, his daughter continues Albert's craft of making banjos and dulcimers.

Because of the promise and interest the younger ones still show hereabout, Thornton and Emily Spencer are cheerfully confident that old-time music will stay in the Virginia highlands for generations yet to come.

Chair Maker

MAX WOODY

HE SPEAKS OF BYGONE DAYS. His voice is clear and his words are crisp—like the wind that sweeps across the cornfields of his beloved Catawba Valley.

"I represent the sixth generation of Woodys who made chairs. My son becomes the seventh. What we do is no guarded family secret. I take people through my shop, and they are hesitant to ask questions. They don't know that I'm just dying to tell them what I know."

Max Woody yearns to keep alive the native crafts. He visits and talks with old people who lived in the days before electricity. From his mountain cabin in the forests above Old Fort he travels to exhibits to meet survivors of the old life, and he listens to ballads and stories. At his shop alongside Clear Creek he shows visitors how his forebears made chairs beginning in the Industrial Revolution. Today, Woody chairs are in homes all over the world. So assured is Max Woody of their lasting value that he will repurchase them for the same money once paid him.

Max was born in 1929 near Glades Creek, which flows northward, joins Crooked Creek, and spills into the Catawba River. It is an area known simply as "The Glades." Max's father, Claude, worked on the railroad with his own father, Martin.

The family once lived in Forest City, but two years before Max's birth there was an accident that was to ravage his future. His hard-laboring father, Claude, pitted his trim body against an enormous freight load and injured his back so badly that he was never again able to stand erect, or lie straight in bed, or lift even moderate loads. He received not a cent of compensation from the railroad, and when finally he left his bed he had to work at simple tasks that paid poorly.

By the time Max was born Claude's condition had deteriorated. He became arthritic, could not hold a common job, and watched his modest accumulations dwindle. Before the misfortune he had owned a Model-T Ford, a paid-for home, new furnishings, and a store of money in a savings account. Now his hard-won nest egg was in hazard. Besides having no income he faced never-ending medical bills.

When at last the home was lost he and his expectant wife put their two young daughters in a friend's truck and went to live near Glades Creek.

In a sparse, new settlement the Woodys hunkered down to unfamiliar labor; they would try to farm. Max's uncles on his mother's side drove over one day from Haywood County. They borrowed a neighbor's mule and plowed the field. After seeding the soil, Max's father bought, on credit, chicks and a milk cow. Soon chickens filled the woods, and the cow begot calves. At last the family began to eat well.

Then the Depression bore down. Granddad Martin, who had worked on the railroad for twenty-one years, was laid off. Unable to find other work, Martin drove up in a truck one day, unloaded his belongings, and moved into Claude's house. Accustomed to having his own way, he became a tyrant at Claude's farm.

"Sell all but one cow," he said. "Except for a few hens, get rid of the chickens. We'll farm this land. If we can't make a go of it we'll move to the cotton mill."

In the back of his mind Martin also might have been thinking of chair making. Years before he went on the railroad he had followed the trade of his ancestors. He made strong chairs and became known as a skilled craftsman throughout the valley. Now he figured he and his crippled son would bring money into the family again. Together they would make chairs.

Martin misreckoned his son's health. The memory of Claude's old productive powers deluded him. In time the old man would need to face facts: Claude's brace was cumbersome; he shuffled about slowly, always in pain, not agile enough to operate the crude machinery. Yet Claude did his best; he had good action remaining in his elbows and wrists; he crafted chairs entirely by hand.

When Granddad Martin finally opened his eyes to the hopelessness he abandoned plans to work with his son. Using credit, he bought two gasoline engines to power

Max Woody, Old Fort, North Carolina

his lathes and other machinery. Then he labored to keep the family afloat. He made and sold chairs. This was the bedrock of his talent, something he could do without dread of being fired.

Martin employed a formula from early American craftsmen. He gathered wood from the forest, shaped it, and crafted chairs that would outlast a human life. He set thoroughly dried rounds into four green posts. The uprights then shrank upon the rounds, forming joints that would endure without screws, nails, or glue.

His own father, Artur, Max's great-grandfather, had made five thousand chairs—square ones with white-oak splits and tall ladder backs and seats of woven wood fiber. It was with Artur that Martin had apprenticed at the end of the last century. Martin had long been a master craftsman, and the years with the railroad had not dulled his skills. He liked to make "mule-eared" chairs; he sold them for a dollar each.

Their farm's bounty put food on the table, but chair sales were not enough to keep the six Woodys from suffering. Finally the mother took a low-paying job at a cotton mill and began working long hours.

The Woodys lived ten miles from the mill, and there was no transportation. Therefore she moved to the mill village to live with her brother's family; to pay her board she cared for the brother's children. On Fridays, when her workweek ended, she boarded a bus and rode home. Her children would be waiting at the bus stop no matter the weather.

Christmas at The Glades ran long and memorable. There was little money for gifts, but the Woodys made the holiday merry. The children would find no toys under the tree, but each would get an apple, an orange, and a tangerine. Yet the aura of the whole season gripped them with wonder. They would go into the forest to chop down a pine. Once they found red and green garlands; these would adorn their tree every year and complement the tinsel they made from the tinfoil of cigarette and gum packages. The mother brought raw cotton from the mill—drab, unbleached lint—and the children smoothed it beneath the tree to simulate snow. They set up the tree at the end of the house's dogtrot—the long hall that divided the sleeping and living areas. At night the children kept the hall door open so that, when dawn broke, they could look from their beds and marvel at the tree's splendor.

Max loved The Glades. He liked to roam the woods and play in the wide fields. He performed light chores and milked the cow in an old log barn. A sister sewed towsacks together to make big sheets. In the fall Max took the sheets into the woods and raked leaves upon them. He then pulled the corners together and gathered large bundles. These he took to the barn and spread high in the stall for the cow's bedding. On frosty mornings and cold evenings he took his pail and sat upon a three-legged stool to milk the cow. The leaves warded off some of the ground chill, and the cow's body warmed the stall. When spring came Max cleaned the stall and strewed the soiled leaves over the garden. Because the Woodys owned no horse or mule, Max broke in a young ox to plow the fields; with the ox he "snaked in" firewood from nearby forests. He was still a child.

At age five Max would slip into his father's toolbox, but when Claude Woody discovered his small son playing with his tools he put a lock on the chest. Then little Max would wait until his father was away. He knocked the pins out of their hinges and opened the case from the back. Briefly the deception worked, but one day Claude came home early. He smiled at the boy's ingenuity but warned him never to go into anyone's private property again. Max continued to work with his hands, an activity that would fascinate him for life.

Max started school in the year the Woodys moved from The Glades. He learned the three R's quickly, and he worked well with his hands. His teacher valued his dedication and encouraged the child.

When he was thirteen Max's family moved five miles north to Marion, and this brought new light into the children's world. "Like Christmas, it was," says Max. "Mama rode to work with a neighbor and came home to us every night."

It was at the new house that Claude enlisted his young son to help bring small change into the household. Claude stashed any extra money in a cigar box. One day there would be enough, he hoped, to make a down payment on a house.

Claude Woody tried to work when others might have chosen to stay in their beds. His arthritic pain was always with him, and he took headache powders to ease it. When he lay on his back his legs bent rigidly in an odd way, so the soles of his feet were angled flat on the bed.

He kept moving by doing light chores. He made statuary alongside his young son, and he knew he must find a way to sell in volume. He built a small runabout in the fashion of a farm wagon. The front wheels were lower than the back, and there was a rocking bolster. A coupling pole shortened and lengthened the wagon as need demanded. When the Woodys carried ordinary loads they used the regular wagon box. For lengthier cargo they extended the coupling pole by removing a pin from one set of holes and placing it in another. It was a handy vehicle for hauling wood, but its main use was in carrying and displaying statuary off the highway.

Motorcars were not yet abundant in the county, and drivers slowed down for the quaint conveyance. Father Claude rode in the wagon bed, his knees resting upon folded towsacks, his hands gripping the sideboards. Young Max, fixing himself between the tongues, drew the rig rickshaw-fashion. He detoured every pebble and crack, because there were no springs to absorb bumps. The father ignored any roughness; he did not complain.

Max would tow his passenger two or three miles at a stretch. When there were hills to climb his father would ask him to stop; he would offer to climb off and walk, but Max would say, "Just let me rest a minute." Then Claude would push his walking cane through the spokes of a front wheel to rough-lock the wagon. When Max was rested they would start anew. If the incline was more than a hundred yards long the boy would pause again to rest.

They would stop along the highway, displaying their statues on boxes. By noon, if they had sold a quarter's worth, Max would walk as far as two miles to buy RC Colas, cans of potted meat, and a nickel box of crackers. "You've no idea how good that was," says Max. "It was a banquet." If they did not sell statues there would be no lunch.

Boys at school had bicycles, but not Max. He was looked down upon because he had no time to play and because he pulled the funny wagon with his kneeling father in its bed. Yet the snobbery did not annoy Max. Steadfastly he stayed with Claude.

"The best times we ever had was then. I'd stop the wagon to rest, and we'd talk. It was good to talk with Dad. And then we'd feel rested and would go back to work, thinking of the things we told each other.

"I was chock-full of love for him, because he put me on his own level. So we'd make those statues, and we'd paint them and pack them in boxes. The next morning I'd get Dad on this little wagon, and we'd go kiting down the highway. We'd stop, display the statues, and wait for people to drive up and browse."

When he was fifteen Max caught a train to Tennessee. He went to a hardwood flooring plant to seek work. The person who hired him did not mention age. The boy was not tall, and his face was without whiskers.

On Christmas Day 1946 Claude Woody suffered a stroke, after which he never spoke again. Max came home from Tennessee and thumbed rides to the hospital at

Rutherfordton. He agonized, watching his gentle father suffer in silence.

"He couldn't speak," says Max, "but he seemed to be having less pain; I took this to mean he was getting better. What he was doing—he was dying."

On the day Max realized his father's life would soon end, he hitched a ride from the hospital and went out to the toolroom in the barn, the place where Claude had built chairs by hand. He looked about, and memories overwhelmed him. The sweet odor of milled lumber and his father's tobacco lingered. He saw Claude smoking and talking, and he wanted to seize time in his hands and hold it. Though Claude was mute and dying, Max reasoned, he was yet *alive*, and perhaps he could remember. The boy hoped that Claude in his pain would be thinking of the times spent with his son at the workbench. Then, as though preparing for his father to come home, Max placed the tools neatly along the bench and oiled each of them.

Word came that Claude was dead, and Max accepted the news grimly. He did not cry. He had wept in his bedroom every night since Christmas. Now that his father's suffering had ended Max began to accept the death. He did not mind that visitors spoke

of his dry eyes. The object in the coffin was no longer his father, he told himself; it was just a body that was empty of soul. Through the night's wake the boy brooded in silence. His thoughts went back to the barn, back to their many talks, back to the little wagon. He dwelled upon the good times.

The night was cold, and the next day icy winds swept down off the Black Mountains. The funeral procession wended its way to the church near the ancestral home of the Woodys. Snow blew horizontally when the pallbearers took the coffin from the church to the grave. A pile of earth lay to the side of a pit that had been dug before the ground froze. The large clods—some the size of a gravedigger's spade—were solid. They lay under a coverlet of tiny white crystals, the kind that fall when it is too cold for large snowflakes.

When the last words were spoken and the chilled mourners turned to leave, men with shovels started to throw the frozen earth upon the wooden coffin. Suddenly the gathering stopped, and heads turned in astonishment. Young Max was running toward the grave. As he ran he held his hands high, signaling the diggers to stop their spading. Then slowly he lowered himself into the pit and began placing the large hunks of frozen earth onto his father's coffin. He could not bear the thuds upon the wooden pall.

When he climbed out the diggers quietly resumed. They drove their spades into the frigid pile, broke open the earthen lumps, and without sound ladled the crumbled bits softly onto the coffin.

Max sat in silence as he rode home in his grandfather's car. The mother and grandmother also were quiet, but Granddad Woody talked. He spoke harshly: "You don't know what work is, boy. You don't know what it is to keep a family alive. If you're ever going to grow up you're already behind time. I don't think you've got it in you."

Max was bewildered. Had he not worked since he was in short pants? What credit was he given for milking the cows, clearing the land, plowing the fields, breaking in an ox, going to work in Tennessee? Had Granddad failed to see there was never an idle moment?

The disconsolate mother did not like the grandfather's attack. She knew the boy did not deserve insults, and she specifically could not understand the old man's unfeelingness at such a time. But neither she nor the boy answered the grandfather. In the way of the times, both respected his patriarchal standing.

"He talked pretty rough to me as we rode back," recalls Max. "But I think I came to understand what that was all about. In later years I figured Granddad was using Br'er Rabbit and the briar patch as a strategy. He was challenging me."

Max thought of his gritty father and remembered that no matter how poor his health he had always worked. Should not he—the young and robust Max—be just as determined? Whole and vigorous, he would apply his father's same dogged will against any odds—even his grandfather's harsh words. He would be worthy.

"I wanted to work like Dad, like Granddad, like my great-grandfather. Didn't know how to start, but I set out to show Granddad and to satisfy myself. What I really wanted was to make chairs—to have my own shop."

Max returned to school that fall, but the flame burned for having his own shop. Academics were only bearable, but in the school's woodshop he found excitement: "My teacher there gave me every opportunity to learn. Even now, when I'm in my shop, those long-ago minutes flash by. I have never yet got tired of working with my hands."

When his last spring term ended Max went to work for sixty-five cents an hour in a furniture factory, never missing a day.

"I wanted that shop."

He hitched rides or walked wherever he went. He owned a mandolin and bought a fiddle; with these he earned money playing at schools and square dances. After three years at the furniture factory he counted his savings. He had eight hundred and fifty dollars.

On a Saturday Max traveled by bus to Charlotte. He went to a hardware store that sold used drill presses, table saws, jointers, and lathes; he carefully chose the items he needed.

When the manager totaled up the bill the boy's euphoria vanished. "It will take everything I've saved in three years to buy this," he said. "Everything."

The manager seemed to feel a kinship. In his office he calculated again and again. When he came out he said that the estimate had been correct. Still, he had a gift: he reduced the price by the amount Max would need to buy lumber for two sets of lawn furniture. The boy could buy the machinery and still have funds left over to get started. Neophyte though he was, it would be easy to make and sell lawn furniture.

"Now," said the man, "bring your truck around."

"I don't have a truck."

The hardware man looked at the boy. He laughed. "I'll send it motor express," he said. "Prepaid."

One afternoon Granddad Martin came by. There were crates spread about the yard, each containing a precious component of Max's planned shop.

"What the hell have you got there?" Granddad Martin asked. He brandished his cane toward the crates.

"Something to build things with," said Max. He searched his grandfather's eyes for a sign of surprise, and what he discovered was a new cordiality. Br'er Rabbit, he sensed, now peeked through the briars.

One summer evening he drove Granddad Martin to Spruce Pine in a borrowed car. They took a few new chairs and visited the chair-making legend known as Uncle Artur.

Max and Martin talked on their return down the mountain. "I'd like to make chairs, Granddad," said Max. "And I'd like only you to teach me."

The following Sunday Max hitched a ride out to his grandfather's house. He stayed there learning to make chairs until he was drafted into the army. A year later in Korea he became a combat engineer.

When Max came home from the war his zeal was even greater. He began to build chairs as his ancestors had. His challenge was to honor his kinsmen by making the best chairs he could.

He built a shop and made a poor living. Then one day a woman from a national magazine came in and bought two rockers. The woman wrote of her purchases and sent Max's address to readers who inquired. Soon orders began coming from throughout the country.

Max moved his shop several times, finally settling on the old Asheville highway, beside Clear Creek, a small stream that flows into the Catawba. It is in the basement of this modest building that Max still makes chairs. On the ground floor, finished chairs fill the showroom; they spill onto the walkway outside.

He watches as his son—a seventh-generation chair maker—works over the ancient lathe. He muses: "I was thinking about the times my dad and I were together. Last night I was thinking about my own sons. Thirty years ago they helped me build my house. One evening we were resting on the side of the hill. The wind was blowing—it was spring—and I told the boys, 'These are golden moments. You don't realize it, but these are times to cherish.'"

Primitive Artist

IN THE TIME AND PLACE of Arlee Mains's youth the only art easily brooked by mountain neighbors was that which was incidental to home crafts. Dabbling in pure art was unknown. To some old-timers, art for art's sake was a frivolity, a devil's plaything—certainly not meant for the austere life of the mountains.

Yet by midcentury new cultures began to steal into the hills. They touched little Arlee Trivette, who grew up in Zionhill on the northwest edge of Watauga County. A passion for art grew within her, and it fairly blossomed as a result of those times when she and playmates—her favorite cousin, Georgie, among them—romped noisily underfoot in adult gatherings.

"When that happened," says Arlee, "the older people would take the bored children out to the barn. There were always corn shucks, and the adults would show us how to use them to make a toy—a dog, a cornstalk horse, a doll. The little girls carried scraps in their pockets; the boys, knives and things. With these we could make figures. We used tree sap for glue, a burnt stick for a pencil. Oh, we maybe had glue and pencils somewhere at home, but it was fun just to use whatever was handy. They'd show us how to put on a doll's eyebrows, its nose. For years I thought that's the way you made faces; then I made my own kind of face later."

Arlee Mains, Boone, North Carolina

Farm animals could not eat cornhusks, so these by-products found limited use as mats for boot wiping, cushion stuffing, and crude hats to ward off the midday sun. Because cornhusks were plentiful Arlee and her playmates were welcome to use them. In their playhouses they kept cornhusk dolls throughout the winter; from elder wood they made flutelike whistles; from prongs of saplings they made slingshots. A store-bought toy was a rarity.

Such was the background of the woman who in time would fuse the private treasures of youth into her life's work.

To Arlee Trivette the world of Zionhill—sometimes called Windy Gap—was a wonder. Its river, its fields, its primitive lanes would be fixed in her mind always. The days with Georgie, Uncle Clark's daughter, were idyllic.

"In terms of childhood I think of Georgie. We spent our complete life together. From very small, we played at some time or other every day. Even if it was bad weather we'd get together and play. Her house was across the field. We didn't think of it as visiting. Georgie was just there, and my other cousins; I was related to just about everybody. They'd come and we'd go home with them—all the cousins I grew up with."

Aunt Ina Hagaman lived in the same rolling countryside. It was she who nudged Arlee into earning money from arts and crafts. Aunt Ina was in her sixties when a federally sponsored program designed to create jobs in Appalachia filtered into the area. Local people made toys such as geehaw-whimmydiddles and items such as hook rugs and birdhouses. They took them to be sold at the craft cooperatives. Aunt Ina, known widely for her old-time skills, welcomed the program. Her first sales were the bright flowers she learned to make as a small girl. In those days she had used paper; now she used cornhusks, the same material from which she once fashioned dolls. She experimented with dyes until she struck upon a kind that would hold its brilliance. She happily showed Arlee her techniques, and soon the two were producing attractive items. They attended craft fairs; they worked at their cottage industry and found outlets for skills that were handed down from bygone years.

Arlee compares the days of the cooperatives to old times: "Before WAMY [a craft cooperative], people didn't get any real money. For a woman who made quilts or hook rugs, there was no place to sell, no tourists to sell to. Until then one shipped up north to somebody that knew a friend that knew a friend that would buy them. A craftsperson would get back maybe five dollars and old clothes and trinkets. Well, that was fine, but it wasn't real money. Mountain people didn't realize they could get real money until WAMY came in and sold to the big stores in New York, and then we all got an income that could mount up to something."

At first Arlee and Aunt Ina had the field to themselves; few others made cornhusk dolls. Soon the aunt was invited to show her dolls at the Smithsonian in Washington. She began to make prettier, more finished dolls. From time to time she wrote the Smithsonian asking that they send her back the old dolls and saying she would return the fancier ones she had begun to make. Arlee remembers that the aunt "got to making them looking like a china doll, not even made from corn shucks." The Smithsonian refused. It would keep the dolls that Aunt Ina thought to be primitive.

"I never did get the hang of it—to make the dolls look like hers," says Arlee. "Mine looked more substantial, hers more delicate. I learnt from her; at the craft fairs she showed me all the little things."

But when Aunt Ina decided she would stop making dolls, Arlee "started having a go at it" all by herself. She developed her own style and created new techniques. She made a new and bigger doll, a different doll. And Aunt Ina viewed Arlee's work with enthusiasm; she continued to encourage her niece.

Neither early nor late in her life did cornhusk dolls satisfy Arlee's restless urge to create. As a girl she drew upon books, brown bags, pulp tablets—"every piece of plunder I could find"—with a penny pencil. She stashed away these sketches, and today she is puzzled as to why she drew so many pictures of underground houses.

"Those drawings were done about the time of the Second World War. Maybe that had to do with things I heard on our battery radio—people going down in the earth to be safe from bombs."

When she was twelve her parents ordered a set of oil paints from Sears-Roebuck. No instructions came with it, but Arlee drew pictures upon the canvas. Each successive drawing covered the other as she tried to unlock the secrets of painting. For all the potential of oils her favorite medium continued to be crayons. She would place her sketches between two pieces of paper and iron over them; the crayons melted into pictures she thought to be beautiful. It was "my favorite thing to do," she says.

Today the primitive oils of Arlee Mains sell faster than she can produce them. She never took a lesson, but she studied any book she could find; she picked up hints; she experimented.

"None of the books suited me—nothing in them I wanted to paint. Finally I got me a great big canvas and a whole bunch of pictures. I painted on that canvas for about a year; every night I would sit and paint out the canvas and paint again.

"Then I found a book that told me about tools in painting—the brush, the paint—everything about the things you use. That helped a lot. Now I could figure out what I was doing. Over and over I painted that canvas. I learned how to paint a tree, a bush, a shrub. That was twenty years ago, and I'm still learning."

In school, teachers admired the girl's work, but they shook their heads: "Arlee, unless you're planning to move from the mountains, you'll never do anything with art. Just forget art; try something else."

It seemed there was always someone around to discourage her. People said that a woman could not succeed in art. Few women, Arlee was told, had ever made anything out of art; it was useless to try.

"Yet my body wouldn't accept that; I wanted to paint, had to paint."

Arlee was obsessed with creating. In the solitude of her room she sketched and painted; she read books; she studied other people's paintings.

"The way they did their paintings did not please me. I didn't want my pictures to look fuzzy. Impressionism. Whatever. I didn't care for pots of flowers. I couldn't relate to that. My mind knew that I needed to paint things I knew about, but I didn't yet realize that. Not really.

"Finally I decided I'm going to paint that old church [on Zionhill] just like I remember it. And that's what I did. When the canvas was finished I liked it. That's what started me to painting like I paint. I paint things I remember."

Having at last found herself, Arlee drew sketch upon sketch, painted canvas after canvas. She called upon childhood memories, and she went beyond. She painted visions fixed in her mind of events that took place before she was born—visions of stories and anecdotes her parents and grandparents told her when she was a child.

Today Arlee calls herself a pack rat. As a child she learned to save every usable thing—strings, rubber bands, brown paper, fertilizer bags. Her mother made aprons, bedsheets, and everyday towels from feed bags. Items were stashed on shelves and in closets. "Nothing laying around," she says. "We used things down to the last scrap." There was no clutter, and that is why her landscapes today are clear and clean.

Despite her frugality there was never enough paper to draw on. Arlee sketched upon books and catalogs, and she painted upon her single canvas until it sagged with oil pigments. Then someone told her she should try painting on wood. She went to her grandfather's fallen-down barn and salvaged shingles—"good, wide shingles, nice, flat, wooden shingles"—and on these she made figures of trolls. "I'd just paint them in several colors, cut them out, and sell them; they sold a lot better than pictures of milk cans or a punkin sitting there."

As she gained income from the troll images, she bought new canvases. Selling potboilers for pocket change was all right, but there was a yearning within her. She must satisfy the soul; she must give vent to a feeling that ran deep.

She began to fill the house with paintings, and later a woman in Banner Elk began to sell her work on consignment. But Arlee kept a few canvases and does not intend to sell them. In one, a snowy mountain slope is dotted sparsely with figures. It grew out of a story told by Miles Ward, her mother's father.

When the grandfather was young, relatives

of his forebears visited from Germany. They told of skiing in the Alps, and this set young minds to work.

"People around here had never skied, you know; they had snowshoes, but no skis," says Arlee. "So the boys in the family decided to make their own skis. They bored holes in long planks and sharpened the ends to make skis. From tree limbs they carved ski poles. When a big snow came they went out—didn't tell their father—and got to going down the hill on those things."

In the tableau there is a litany of mini-events: a girl in an ankle-length dress skiing primly out of harm's way; a child's sled in descent; a grandfather at the base of the slope, arms gesticulating in reproach; and neophyte skiers in various attitudes of tumbles and pratfalls. One of the boys—Council Harmon by name—slips backward, legs flailing, skis splintering, poles breaking. Council was an inveterate entertainer. He told stories and sang songs. Long after he died, folklorist Richard Chase immortalized him in books of Jack Tales and Grandfather Tales.

Although Harmon and his brothers put away thoughts of skiing, each generation since has heard the story and tried its luck on the slopes of Windy Gap. "First my mother and her brothers," says Arlee. "Then me'n Georgie. We did good, though; we didn't break anything."

Arlee is proud that she has Indian blood and the dark eyes and dark hair of Indians. Her mother was a Ward. There were those among the family who married Cherokees; the famous Indian Nancy Ward was a distant relative. Arlee thinks that, together, the white and red people of the mountains had a commonality: they were known for hiding.

"They [the government] drove the Indians out, made them march to Oklahoma. But a few hid in the hills, and a lot of people here were friendly to them. People in the mountains were rebels, too. Many had run off from the coast. Most were bonded servants. They decided they weren't going to serve their terms, and they escaped to the mountains. So mountain people were like the Indians; they were hunted, too."

When playing cowboys and Indians as a girl Arlee always chose to be an Indian. She insisted, too, that the Indians win their share of playground wars.

"We were always partial to the Indians in my family; that maybe says why I have such a fascination with the Native American culture."

In her den Arlee works most of the day at painting and crafts. She rotates her tasks, working alternately at paintings, dolls, wall hangings, miniature quilts, and Indian crafts.

She does this to avoid burnout, she says. Among her favorite tasks is creating a thing called a dreamcatcher.

"It's a web Indians used," she says. "Not Cherokees—Oneida Indians, probably. I learned about it at a powwow over in Tennessee. An old Indian said that a long time ago it was learned that whoever slept around spider webs had good dreams, didn't have bad dreams. Well, they moved around, you know, and whenever they moved camp the spiders didn't go along to make webs wherever needed. So there would be bad dreams. Then some medicine man made himself a spider web of his own. Wove it like they wove snowshoes and little baskets. He blessed this, his own spider web, and hung it up. It worked. All the bad dreams would get caught in the web, but the good dreams went through the middle hole and would drop down and give good dreams."

Arlee explains that when a child was born its parents wove for it a plain dreamcatcher. As the child grew they added trinkets—fetishes that were meant to make a good dream come true. "It was filtering away the bad dreams and letting the good dreams come right through. That's what a dreamcatcher is. A child kept it for life."

Another piece on her wall is a charm called a mandella. It was used, she says, as a kind of horseshoe for good luck. The Indians hung large ones in dwellings and carried small ones on horses or tied them to shields or spears. Arlee's mandella is built around a raccoon head. "It should have been a bear's head," says Arlee. "But I can't get a bear's head, can't even get bear claws anymore." So Arlee sculpts the claws from clay.

Her life's resolve "to make something" is now realized. It extends well beyond the walls of her home, which sits off a lane at the end of a deep slope. In her crowded den she creates primitive paintings out of old times; she crafts cornhusk dolls and three-dimensional needlecraft. She then loads the harvest of her labor and takes it to craft centers and art galleries. Besides feeding a primal hunger to create, she likes knowing that her products are in far-off homes. She likes being where a childhood passion has taken her.

"But my husband says, 'You're beginning to make something of it, now that you're too old.'

"Which is true," Arlee says, "but I don't think much about it. When you get sixty you begin to wonder."

She can barely get into her workroom, she says, because of the piles of arts-and-crafts materials she has crammed into it.

"My husband tells me I won't live long enough to use the stuff I've packed. And I say, 'I know that, but just in case . . .'"

$\mathcal{S}torekeeper$

IN SUMMER AND FALL they come to Valle Crucis from many places. They browse through Old Mast Store and bask in a time that moves like the patient tick of an ancient clock.

While welcoming their visitors, inhabitants such as Howard ("H.") Mast decry the surrender of the village to profit. Nothing or nobody, they fear, will come along to temper the defilement.

From his living room H. Mast gazes out over the lawn toward the road that runs through the flat valley. Directly across is a second Mast outlet, called The Annex; it was once operated by his wife's parents. Slowly he shakes his head.

"We sensed what was happening, saw it coming years ago. Some of us tried to stop it with zoning laws. But people in our church and close relatives told us we weren't going to tell them what to do with their land. Said they were going to sell the land if they wanted to."

H. Mast acknowledges that this is the don't-tell-me-what-to-do spirit of mountain pioneers, and that now it has come back to haunt the great valley. Whereas peacefulness and love of land cause even the neediest in the North Carolina settlements of Laurel Creek and

H. Mast, Valle Crucis, North Carolina

Rominger to hold onto their titles, a few heirs around Valle Crucis have allowed their homeplaces to be sold. Developers buy tracts on the mountainsides and in the river basin; they sell to well-meaning outsiders who want to claim experiences from the old life. But H. Mast says that, to the dismay of many families, every added shop, every new structure taints the wonderment of the setting.

From the entry road that winds above the valley, the long view is that of rural Europe.

Close up is where the deterioration begins to reveal itself. When H. Mast looks upon the encroachment he remembers the Valle Crucis of his younger days. He does not like to think of what the village will become.

Those who want to live here, he concedes, have dreams of sharing the glory of the old days. Less than two decades ago Valle Crucis was a quiet place where sheep and cows roamed broad pastures. There were fields of corn and bottom lands that were among the richest in the mountains; there were big houses and barns. Nobody ever reckoned that New Yorkers and Floridians would come searching for a home here.

Natives who hold to their land agree with H. Mast that when charm yields to growth Valle Crucis will become an ordinary tourist trap, and its precious quality will be no more.

When in 1780 David Hicks (or Hix) staked a claim to hundreds of acres of bottom land here, his family became one of the first to settle the fertile ground through which flow the Watauga River and three meandering creeks. According to local history, after Hicks died, an heir swapped three hundred acres of his legacy for a few dollars, a hog rifle, a sheep's hide, and a white-and-tan dog. The old ones say that in those early days it was a reasonable deal, since a good hog rifle was harder to come by than land.

In the middle of the nineteenth century, after Episcopalians set up a mission school, the area became known as Valle Crucis, which is Latin for Vale of the Cross—so called, some say, because Pigeonroost, Clark, and Dutch Creeks met to shape the image of a crucifix. A great flood in 1940 changed that configuration, and today there is little evidence to confirm the story.

Bishop Levi Ives later started a school for women that attracted students from all over the East. The school has long been closed, but a church and a retreat on its former property survive.

Farther down the valley, Old Mast Store thrives as a tourist attraction and post office. It is a de facto museum. Its floors are creaky and its walls are warped. Its merchandise no longer draws the farm trade; rather, its goods are rustic—colorful sweaters, canvas pants, rugged boots, topographic maps, backpacks, jams, and jellies.

For H. Mast memories of the old store tarry. He thinks of the time when he was barely tall enough to see over the counter. The store was then a place for farmers and herb gatherers, men and women who brought plants to sell or barter: ginseng, red and black cohash, cherry bark, witch hazel, peppermint, spearmint, catnip, angelica, queen of the meadow, mayapple, and lobelia. He recalls that the most expensive herb was ginseng.

"They'd come in and say, 'I went a-hunting today.' And you'd say something like, 'Get any ginseng?' And they'd likely say, 'No, but I got some 'sang.' On the mountain they could recognize ginseng instantly, but they knew it only as 'sang."

Henry Taylor founded the store well over a hundred years ago. Then in 1897 H. Mast's grandfather William Wellington Mast bought an interest; customers began to know the place as Taylor & Mast General Merchandise. In 1913 Taylor sold his part, after which the business was informally known for many years as "Will Mast's old store."

It is difficult to imagine how mountain people lived in that time. After they paid their bills at harvest there was little money. Until the next harvest they ran credit for tools and seeds and implements needed to farm their land. They bartered for sugar, coffee, shoes, and even caskets for their dead, bringing their herbs, chestnuts, eggs, butter, and animal hides to trade. It was not unusual for an entire family to go through the winter with less than three dollars stashed in the cupboard.

Old-timers of the hills still speak of H.

Mast's grandfather in fondness. Although their trade made Will Mast well off they seem to begrudge him nothing. His enterprise minimized their impoverishment. He knew them by name, extended credit willingly, and allowed them to barter the products of their labor. If there was no money Will Mast would accept in trade a horse or cow or hog. Often an animal was raised with the idea of paying off a debt to the Mast Store the following year.

"I may have been poor," a Spice Branch farmer recalls, "but I never went owing."

H. Mast's grandfather stocked only the items his customers needed, and he bartered only for goods he could sell to other customers and to wholesalers in Boone. It was a mutuality that brought benefits—if only meager ones.

In its time the Mast Store was to local residents what downtown was to urban people. Rarely did the hill people come to Valle Crucis in a car or even on the back of a mule. They walked; they carried flour sacks containing hides of muskrat, mink, opossum, weasel, and raccoon; they brought herbs, dried beans, chestnuts, and molasses. H. Mast and his fellow clerks would sprinkle the hides with salt, roll them tightly for curing, and later put them up for sale. When country people brought goods in their flour sacks, they would reload the same sacks with bartered-for items—denim cloth, shoes, refined flour, tins of sardines, coffee, sugar—and trek back over Long Mountain with the sacks on their backs.

In later years people would drive up from Boone, Lenoir, Hickory, Wilkesboro, and towns in Tennessee. They came for the store's renowned "hog hams." For many years the Masts bought hams from farmers, cured the hams, and sold them to nonfarm customers. The meat was raised locally, and the curing was from a recipe closely guarded by H. Mast's family. The hams were never smoked; the ingredients had a salt base. For many years, long after H. Mast's father—the elder Howard—had taken over the store, standing orders were kept in a ledger.

Often customers would ask for a twelve- or fifteen-pound ham, but the storekeepers would urge them to buy a twenty- or twenty-five-pounder. H. Mast says the customers would agree to the suggestion. The bone in a large ham was not much bulkier than in a small one. "They'd get more meat for their money," he explains. For this reason the Masts bought big hams whenever they could. "Once we bought one that weighed sixty-five pounds."

The popularity of their product became so widespread that the Masts could not get enough hams for even their best customers—those they had sold to for many years.

"Then the government came along and said we couldn't cure any more hams as we'd been doing. They wanted us to have a sanitation rating, and that meant having both hot and cold running water. We'd never had hot water in the store, you know. Also they were going to inspect us regularly before we could cure and resell the hams."

So, in the spirit of mountain independence, the Masts decided against changes and against government inspectors. There were sad customers when the owners at last stopped buying, curing, and selling hams.

Other than their churches, the Mast Store was the single most important institution in the lives of pioneers from Egg Knob, Spice Branch, Beech and Laurel Creeks, Matney, Kellerville, and even as far as Dark Ridge. Saturday was a big day; farmers would jam the store. But in the fifties they began to pile into pickups and go to Boone, reducing the crowds. Still there were the checker-playing, stove-huddling faithful who stayed late spinning tales of fox hunting, coon hunting, and fishing. That was before electric lines invaded the mountains, and they would walk home in the dark. They did not care to depart early because, as H. Mast remembers, "there was no television to go home to."

Old Will Mast often told his customers, "If we ain't got it you don't need it." Indeed he anticipated the needs of people in two counties. He kept farm equipment—mowing machines, hay rakes, plows, disks. If a farmer broke a piece of machinery he could be sure that a replacement would be found at the store.

Will Mast hired local people to help, part-time clerks whose main work was on the farm. When the store became overly busy he would send to certain farms for help. It was a good arrangement; helpers could earn cash that was not otherwise easy to come by. If Will Mast failed to get a full quota from the farms there was always a reservoir of kinfolk to draw upon.

H. Mast was born in Boone. When he was six years old he came to Valle Crucis with his parents. As a first- or second-grader he began helping the busy clerks. He sold items like candy and even work shoes. He loved the place and soon began working there anytime he could.

In 1939 Will Mast retired and sold the store to a likable New Englander, a quick, bright, and hardworking man whom H. Mast remembers was "not a moneymaking merchant." At last the man sold the store to Howard Mast—a son of Will Mast and the father of H. Mast. In 1952 the store's name was changed to Howard W. Mast, Incorporated.

H. Mast and his mother joined a few outside clerks, and together they helped Howard operate the store. But paved roads and electricity were now common in the rural communities; local farmers owned pick-ups and old cars; they made their way into Boone, where grocers bought in bulk and sold at prices the Masts could not afford. And television came into many remote cottages and cabins. Soon the venerable store no longer was central to back-road settlements along the Watauga River.

Howard Mast suffered poor health much of his life. In his early teens he had fallen through the opening where hay was stored in a barn. His hip was fractured, but his pride would not let him tell his parents. The injury mended during the next few months, but because the bones were not set right the boy was lamed permanently; his damaged leg grew an inch shorter than the healthy one. Through his remaining years he wore a built-up shoe. Seven or eight years before he died he underwent a hip replacement and regained a bit of length, but by then his health was gone.

In 1971, having worked in the store for nearly thirty years, Howard Mast retired, and his son H. Mast became its operator.

"There were two telephones in the store," the younger Mast remembers. "One was called the local line, and anybody who wanted into Valle Crucis got the party line. Then we had a Bell Telephone line, and the mission school and Episcopal church had the other. Sometimes we'd get long-distance phone calls. Maybe a boy in service in California wanted to get word to his parents.

Any kind of a message, and we'd deliver the information."

In winter neighbors would call on the local line, saying, "My truck won't start. Come on over here and boost me off." And H. Mast would go through the snow in a pickup truck with four-wheel drive. He'd go anywhere in Watauga and Avery Counties with his booster cables. If a disabled vehicle would not respond he'd affix a tow chain and pull the car to get it started. If there was a fire in the community the victims might call the store and ask, "Anybody down there that can help put out a fire?"

"Yessir," says H. Mast. "Today that store would have to shut down if it depended on local trade. It's now all transient. Back in our day outsiders were just the icing on the cake."

He remembers they had visitors who often stayed the summer.

"My grandmother kept boarders, they were called. And the Taylor House, the Mast Farm Inn, and the Shull House up here all kept these boarders. They had regular people who came up each summer for a week or two, mostly people from Charlotte or Greensboro or Lincolnton, someplace fairly close, but a few from Florida."

The visiting children would play by the river and roam the hills. They liked to go out into the valley to see the sheep and up on the hills to watch the cattle graze, and to ride the horses and ponies kept by farmers.

"That's the way the valley sorta ran back then. Local people would come and help each other; they'd swap a day's work for a day's work. Some of the boarders would go to the farms: 'You got melons or sweet corn?' and 'You got a ham you can sell me?' or 'Sell me a dozen ears of sweet corn, and those tomatoes look good.' See, the farmers got something directly from the boarders coming up here."

Contemporary living crept into the valley in many ways. As old homesteading families died off and their heirs sold off pieces of the farms, there were monied newcomers who were delighted to buy land, build homes, and come to Valle Crucis for the summer. As outsiders invaded they brought pets that often roamed with wild dogs. In the fifties sheep raisers finally gave up. They found it impractical to raise lambs because of the increased number of killer dogs.

H. Mast still goes to the store and sorts mail into post-office boxes. Though there are a few survivors from the old days, he remembers when customers from remote places would come to the store carrying sacks that, when filled, would bend their backs deeply. The bags were closely woven, so even tiny grass seeds would not sift through—white, hundred-pound sacks that the mountain people would fill with flour, meal, lard, sugar, or coffee.

There are some still living who remember the vitality of the old store. Said an old man from Stone Mountain, "My son took me there a few years ago, and the store didn't look much different. But the things they sell ain't like before. Different ones coming in. I'd speak to some, and they'd just look at me. It's a real nice store, but I reckon times have passed me by."

Blacksmiths

 UNDER NORTH CAROLINA'S LOFTY BLACK MOUNTAINS, an anvil rang down the streets like the peal of a church bell. It summoned the small boy Bea Hensley and haunted him; it would reverberate always in his memory.

Bea came to Burnsville with his family when he was four. The Hensleys relocated there so the father, a Baptist minister, could study at the Yancey County Institute. They moved across the street from the Boone family, and before long little Bea became acquainted with Daniel Boone VI, descendant of the famed trailblazer. It was the anvil of Daniel's father that lured young Bea in those tail-end days of shoeing horses and fixing wagons. By Bea's reckoning there was at that time a blacksmith shop at every road fork.

The younger Daniel and his brothers Wayne and Lawrence took up where their father left off, following the trade of their forebears. As time passed their enterprise seemed doomed. In the way of the buggy whip, common blacksmithing had begun to vanish from the American scene. Town and farm customers found that buying new equipment was easier and cheaper than fixing the old.

It was Daniel VI who led the way to his family's recovery. He regretted the passing of a time-honored trade that he, his father, and his brothers had mastered. How could their life's work be saved?

Infrequently the Boones had been asked to make iron gates, screens, fire sets, and they had obliged their neighbors. He wondered, If we make these products better than people can buy them elsewhere, will the business come?

Coincidentally there arose a general interest in ornamental ironwork around that time. Daniel began to order equipment for fancy blacksmithing. Lees-McRae College at Banner Elk got in touch with Daniel. With his father and brothers Daniel taught students ironworking. All the Boones buckled down to perfect an enhanced trade. Two years later they returned home, and Daniel built a large shop in Burnsville.

Bea Hensley remembers with clarity: "I was old enough to watch him, but I was sort of in awe of Daniel. He was about the best blacksmith you'd ever see. I wanted to work in iron, but I knew I'd never be as good as Daniel."

Then soon after finishing high school Bea talked with a minister; somehow it came out that he secretly wanted to work in iron.

"Go over there and tell that to Daniel," said the minister. "Tell him you want to work with him."

The next day Bea went over to Daniel's shop.

"Daniel, what about working some with you?"

"Well sure, Bea. Come on in."

In the weeks and months afterwards Bea worked long hours; he listened and observed.

"It was from that, working with Daniel—he was such a good teacher—that I started getting the confidence."

Bea helped with routine chores. Daniel, in whatever spare time he had, would show the boy the knives, hatchets, and axes he had crafted. He would say that if Bea could learn to make those items he could call himself a blacksmith.

Bea indeed had found his calling. The anvil's clangor and the smells and warmth of the blacksmith's shop harmonized with his enormous energy. But when World War II began, iron sources for commercial uses dried up, and the ornamental trade was stilled. So Bea packed his tools and moved up the highway to Spruce Pine. He joined Gunter Machine Company—"one of the finest machine shops in the country," he says. Before long he was made foreman of twenty-eight machinists, and he remained with the company for eight years after the war. The shop served firms that mined feldspar, mica, and other minerals from the mountains around Spruce Pine.

In his years with Gunter, Bea became skilled with lathes, milling machines, planers, and other kinds of instruments. He was happy that his career had taken such a turn; he delayed thoughts of going back to blacksmithing. Then a serious accident changed his future with Gunter; it caused him to wonder if he would ever work again.

"A latch came loose on a big load, and it came down and hit my welding helmet, laid me down into the ground. It was a long time before I could hear the birds sing again. For seventeen months I was in and out of the hospital. The accident nearly separated my spine from my brain."

His body mended with agonizing slowness, but Bea needed to make a living. He purchased an acre of land off U.S. 221 within a stone's throw of the Blue Ridge Parkway; he built a cinder-block shop and opened a blacksmith operation similar to but smaller than his friend Daniel's down at Burnsville.

He could barely wait to get started. The first day, he opened his new shop at dawn, while most of his friends were still in their beds. By normal opening time he was seeing double and stumbling about. The excitement, the sixteen pills a day he was taking, the hurrying of his recovery—all seemed to bear down upon him. Closing the shop's doors, he put his head on his desk and waited for the swimmy feeling to leave him. Then, the doors still closed, he got up from his seat and drew plans until dizziness overtook him again. Finally his "spells" subsided, and Bea walked to the doors and opened

them. He was astonished to see people milling about outside.

"Well, Bea," said one, "we been a-waiting for you to get back to work."

Bea, his eyes crinkling, smiles to remember: "From that day on the business just took off."

Bea's son Mike played around the shop from the time he was old enough to walk. At four he began helping—cleaning fire sets, andirons, and screens, all the while observing his father at work. At school he told his teacher that he wanted to become a blacksmith, and she knew instantly that he was serious. To Bea it soon became evident that not only was Mike being trained, but that his output was becoming useful. The boy was learning that one must know how to finish a piece before beginning one.

At seven he had already gained his father's confidence. If Bea happened to be out of the shop when a customer walked in with an order, Mike would quote a price. If later the customer questioned Bea about the estimate, Bea would say, "That's the cost, then." Although Mike might at times quote too low a price his father never questioned him. It was his unique way of helping his son develop into a responsible businessman.

As a small boy Mike thought of

blacksmithing as a game. "To me it wasn't work. Learning the language of the anvil was play. I didn't realize how much I was learning."

Still, at the age of nine, Mike was fast becoming a partner to his father.

"I think that by his putting so much trust in me, forcing me to deal with the public, he was training me to be a far better blacksmith. Dad would tell me, 'Your work doesn't have to be bought, but it will be if you make a better product.' He said that when I did a job I should look for all that's bad in it and correct the bad, because, he said, the good will take care of itself."

Father and son agreed early that they should be candid about each other's work.

"When I was six or seven Dad would say, 'Come over here and look. Tell me what's wrong with this.' He asked my opinion often. We didn't work together as father and son—more as joint owners. I always had the most respect for him, and still do. He's seventy-five and I'm forty-eight. We still give each other a hug every once in a while."

The reputation of Bea and his son began

Bea Hensley, Spruce Pine, North Carolina

to spread. They made it plain that they were not mass producers, but rather artisans who designed and crafted single pieces, whether reproductions or originals. When officials of Colonial Williamsburg ordered forty thousand reproductions, the Hensleys wrote back, "We can't count that high."

On the other hand, they dug deep into their store of talents to make individual copies. The McRaes of Linville talked with them; they wanted to reproduce a single room from the McRae castle in Scotland; they needed smaller versions of the castle's chandeliers. From a picture, Bea and Mike designed and crafted the heavy fixtures. Years before they had fashioned three large chandeliers for a building at the Great Lakes Naval Training Center.

Until his death Daniel Boone VI remained a cherished friend to Bea. He often visited the Spruce Pine shop; if he developed some new technique he would share it with Bea. "I taught you to do it this way," he might say. "I'd been doing it this way for fifty years, but now here's a better way, and maybe you will want to try it." Bea contends that the long association with his old friend made him known widely. There has never been a day in Bea's enterprise when projects have not waited.

"The world comes here," says son Mike.

"We're right behind the Mineral Museum, as close to the parkway as you can get. In fact this line [he draws an imaginary boundary outside] marks the parkway right of way."

A visitor may hear the sound of the anvil and wander over from the Mineral Museum. Some make contracts on the spot; others pass the word back home, which sometimes results in orders.

"We stay busy; we deal with a lot of people from places we never even heard about," says Bea. "But we're home people. This is where we live. When a boy comes in with a pedal broke off his bicycle I'll stop whatever I'm doing and fix it. Free. I put a lot more emphasis on living than on making a living."

Although Bea has been known to arise at three in the morning and work past dusk, he paces himself, never seeming to forget his passion for a full life. He is sure that his accident of many years ago changed him.

"Life is short," he says. "You can be out of it in a minute, and I realize that. I never let the accident bother me, because I went ahead and did my work. But it changed my perspective a whole lot.

"Mike and I'll sometimes pack up our fly rods and leave here about five-thirty or six—"

"Or maybe even five or five-thirty," interrupts a waggishly chiding son.

Bea smiles wryly. "Well, maybe that, occasionally. We'll go to Linville River and start throwing in our lines. There's nothing in the world that will relieve the stress of your mind like trout fishing."

Bea's considerable energies are spent upon family, religion, iron crafting, and angling. Into the latter two he enfolds another passion—a concern and respect for youth. After repairing a toy for one child Bea might teach another how to tie flies. He allows—actually encourages—young ones to watch him work in the forge.

"Oh, Dad will get down on his knees to talk with kids," says Mike. "He believes you've got to be at children's eye level, so they can understand you."

He tells a story. In the fifties a minority family from New York stopped their Cadillac at the forge; they were lost and needed directions. As Mike drew a map for the tourist father, Bea appeared. He saw a small boy and girl in the car with their mother and hurried out to greet them. Taking the children in his arms, he brought them into the shop and showed them how he worked in iron. When the father gathered his little ones to leave he turned and smiled. "Where are all the bad people?" he asked.

The forge harbors memories. Hardly a week passes when people do not stop by to call up the good times of a generation ago. They talk of how Bea Hensley trained one to strum a guitar, showed one how to tie a fishing fly, or took one fishing off the parkway.

"They must be given the basics," says Bea. "They must learn not to throw the fly in the wind, but walk up to a pool and throw into the middle of the swirl, where the foam is, where trout most likely feed."

Bea's "alumni" drift in all through the summer. On one typical day two doctors, one after the other, drop by to visit.

The first is a plastic surgeon at the Mayo Clinic—"an old country boy from Spruce Pine," he says.

Bea, who rarely frowns, breaks out in a wide grin; he says the surgeon's visit is "the best thing that's happened in forty-eight hours." The visitor tells Bea he's taking welding lessons, and Bea tells him he will live a lot longer by doing that.

"I think so," says the physician. "Welding's a lot like fishing; it doesn't count against real time."

After the surgeon leaves, a doctor comes in from Danville, Virginia. He's another who spent hours at Bea's forge in his youth. "I kind of grew up here," he says.

Mike says he was a benefactor of his father's natural liking for children. It was his father's easy, equal treatment of children that molded Mike's career and his way of looking at life.

Mike: "We've always gone places together. We fish and camp all over these mountains. God's beauty."

Bea: "From the time he was eight or nine we'd go and camp out in the Smoky Mountains. There's one stream we like to fish, called Slick Rock Creek. Between North Carolina and Tennessee, down toward Chattanooga. At four o'clock we'd get up and walk as hard as we could to see the sunrise."

Mike: "We'd go in to Slick Rock. Take about four hours to walk in there. Walk two miles down by the lake and cut up a long, beautiful valley. Yellowhammer Gap. There was a spring in there that, as Dad says, we'd rush to get to. A pure stream."

Bea: "The sun came up over the peak and shined down into it. And it was the strangest thing—never figured out what happened, but out of that spring, right at daylight, a cross, a crucifix, would rise."

Mike: "We mean a physical cross, which you could see through the sunlight. It'd come straight up out of the pit of that spring and rise right up into the air."

Bea: "It was perfect. Didn't have to use your imagination. It would come out pretty. Floated right up. I tell you, I think about it. It'll make you look deep into life."

Though father and son have lived their whole existence in the highlands they are always in awe of mountain nature. There are phenomena that baffle and delight them, but they are not curious to know the whys.

They are amused by the varied reactions outsiders have to the inexplicable Brown Mountain Lights, a frequent spectacle nearby that scholars have attempted to explain since the nineteenth century.

Bea: "A lot of people make fun of it. They just don't know."

Mike: "I've seen it look like a fence rail afire on top of that mountain. I've seen red, blue, and white lights. One night coming out of Connelly Springs, where we used to fish a lot, we watched a red one about the size of a car's headlight. It came off the mountain, up from the top and over the edge and down the end of the gorge, down the river and back out."

Bea: "I mean, you didn't have to strain to see it."

Mike: "Too fast-moving for a human. Just moving in the air."

Bea: "One night we were coming out of Wiseman's View, and it was kind of scary. One came out right across—"

Mike: "Out of Table Rock. It traveled in a straight line and right across toward us. It was blue."

Bea: "You don't have to worry about car lights or lights coming from human sources.

I don't care what anybody says. It's there. The best time to see the lights is right after an electrical storm. That mountain goes *z-z-z-z-z*. I mean, it lights up like a bunch of sparklers. That red light we saw came after a storm; it must have been three feet across."

Knowledge of the Hensleys' skills ranges far. Once a University of Michigan official talked to Bea about coming there to teach; orders from Sturbridge Village, Williamsburg, and even Augusta National Golf Club come regularly; and in September 1995 Bea went to Washington for a week to accept a National Heritage Award.

Though he is a national treasure he is unaffected by recognition. It is not easy to know when his work is play and when play is work; he seems deeply intrigued and happy in either.

When years ago someone claimed Bea "could play a tune on that anvil," the old artisan set out to make it actually happen. Now in his shop he will take a drill rod (off a jackhammer) and a common hammer. Through hundreds of trials he has succeeded in tuning the two instruments against the anvil so that the notes are in harmony. He will play a specially composed tune for his listeners, who will find the percussive sounds haunting.

$\mathcal{P}$layactor

On a June morning in 1954 the late Kai Jurgensen—drama professor and director of Kermit Hunter's outdoor production, *Horn in the West*—drove out to the Austin homestead on Winkler's Creek. He had come from Chapel Hill only the night before, and soon he would launch rehearsals for the drama's third year. Today he wanted to talk with the young man who would again play the role of Daniel Boone. Jurgensen regarded Ned Austin as the progeny of the real mountain frontier people. The actor's forebears had come to the North Carolina mountains from Pennsylvania in the late 1700s, about the same time Daniel Boone's family arrived and settled on the not-too-distant Yadkin River.

Even before reaching the Austin homestead Jurgensen spotted a figure on a steep hillside, a young man laboring behind a mule and turning plow. The professor stopped his car, stepped out into the spring breeze, and breathed deeply the scent of freshly tilled soil. He did not call out but waited for Ned to reach the end of a curved row. Ned finagled the mule to begin another row and then saw Jurgensen. Sunburned and dark bearded, he smiled broadly and left his plow. His teeth gleamed, his hair shone healthily, and he stepped down sideways over the new furrows. He did not seem as large as the Daniel Boone of legend, but his rugged body, his direct look, his clear greeting seemed to issue from a distant past.

He kept the broad smile as he pulled out a bandanna and wiped his bronzed forehead. He shook hands and talked easily, comfortably. This Ned, this actor-plowman, spoke with an eloquence Jurgensen thought belonged only to the old orators like Abraham Lincoln. He knew Ned to be of no little sophistication—a man who drank fine wines, kept up with world events, and read liberally. He studied dramatists—from Shakespeare to Shaw to Ibsen to Tennessee Williams to Arthur Miller. He read, too, the most poetic books of the Bible.

In just two weeks rehearsals would end; on opening night the stage's Daniel Boone would speak lines attributed to the real pathfinder; the words would seem to cross a bridge of centuries.

Ned's family did not approve his acting. His forebears had farmed along Winkler's Creek since before the nation came to be. Young Ned had honored that austere life, that Dutch-German and English farm heritage; he worked hard and memorized Scripture; he tried to please.

The elder Austins were bright and industrious, but like so many rural folk of the day they could not read. Yet they understood the Bible. Ned's mother was the daughter of an old-time Baptist preacher. When she was a little girl she would go to the well to get water; out of sight of others she would pray that God would give her a preacher. One day when she was grown and married she told the boy Ned that from her brood she had chosen him to be that preacher.

Months later, at a revival meeting up at Poplar Grove, Ned was overwhelmed by an evangelist's fervor. When the call came for those who wanted to accept Jesus as their Savior, the boy—not quite sure he was saved—made his way to the mourners' bench. After all, he reasoned, he was destined by his mother's prayers to spread the gospel.

That night Ned's sisters came down the aisle and prayed over him, but he kept wondering, If I'm really saved, shouldn't something happen? He felt nothing except the lingering fear of the preacher's words and the need to conform to the ways of God-fearing parents. He expected to hear a voice or receive some sign to confirm his faith; when nothing came he tried mightily to understand how a saved person should behave.

Ned's older brothers and sisters had attended a one-room school in Poplar Grove, but when he came along there was a consolidated school at Boone. He was to discover that, coming from a farm, he was not among the socially accepted. Like others from the country Ned felt he was looked down upon, and the bright, sensitive child from Winkler's Creek bore the stigma in silence.

Nonetheless, as time went by, Ned learned to thrive in his second-class role. Back at the farmhouse at night the boy would enlist a sister to read to him. The next day he would mesmerize schoolmates with tales learned from the encyclopedia.

Perhaps because of his stage presence he played the groom in a Tom Thumb wedding one May Day. The event took place on the college campus at Boone, and the attention of the friendly audience, Ned felt,

was fastened upon him. When he heard their laughter and applause he sensed an addiction for the stage taking hold.

On the other hand, there was a vague unrest. In the weeks following, his moral nature tugged at him; his country raising told him that drama was foolish and impractical. For these reasons he tried to push playacting from his mind. But the lure of theater persisted; it became a powerful temptation for one whose mother had asked God to give her a preacher son.

After high school he was accepted to study pre-law at Mars Hill College near Asheville. But World War II came, and be-

Ned Austin, Winkler's Creek, North Carolina

fore long Ned enlisted in the Air Corps. Later, as he prepared to go into pilot training, he and thirty thousand others received a message that the Air Corps would need fewer pilots; he was then pressed into the infantry.

In 1945 the boy from Winkler's Creek was captured on the Rhine River about twenty kilometers from Koblenz; he spent the remainder of the conflict in a German prison camp.

After the war Ned returned to college. The more he learned about law the less interested he became. He then applied by letter and was accepted into summer stock in Surrey, Maine.

Back at Winkler's Creek, Ned happily announced the news. His family's reaction stunned him. If he'd told them he was going to prison it would have been no different. His smile withered before a wintry silence. It came upon him that his loved ones saw him forsaking his upbringing and taking up a life of sin. His mother, father, sisters, and brothers gathered around and prayed for him.

Today he looks back ruefully: "I wish I could say it didn't affect me, but it did."

After Surrey and a summer of acting in New York stock productions, strange things began to happen. Although one director and then another saw the potential of the young mountain man, Ned became physi-

cally ill each time he was called for a trial performance.

"I wasn't afraid I'd not get the part," he says. "I was afraid I would."

He tried to stay with the theater, to overcome a deeply embedded ethic that said acting was sinful. Yet no matter where he went in drama his conscience challenged the reasonableness of his acts. He wondered if he could escape the demon dreams of acting by becoming a preacher.

"Probably not," he says now. "I'd have dreamed about the stage. Wondered what it was like. I didn't believe what the preachers believed, you see. Never did. Never believed that stuff about hellfire and heaven. It doesn't mean I'm an atheist, understand; I just never bought those things the preachers said."

As a child in Sunday school Ned had once talked of tomorrow and how God knew what would happen.

The teacher interrupted and said, "No, God doesn't know what we're going to do tomorrow."

Ned said, "Miss Ethel, he just has to."

He had gone home and talked to his mother: "Mama, Miss Ethel doesn't believe that God knows what we're going to do tomorrow."

And his mother had shaken her head and

said, "He really doesn't."

The momentum turned against Ned's becoming a preacher. Increasingly the God of the Baptist church in the valley played against the God of the little boy's perception. How was he to become a preacher when he was at odds with the established church and its many believers?

Yet throughout his youth he never went to sleep without first reading, by the light of an oil lamp, the lyrical verses of Psalms and Proverbs.

Did the Bible itself confer his gift of drama?

"No. I tell you what: I think I always had a flair. Before I can remember, they had called me Silas. See, back in the Depression, people would come and stay a week or so, or until their welcome got frayed a little, and then they'd move on to somebody else's house. Our house seemed to be one of those places where both kin and strangers would come.

"One day, my people said, an old man with a white beard and cane knocked at the door. They tell me he said, 'I don't guess you know me, but my name is Silas Findley.' And my folks had him in. Meantime, they said, I went around to the front and knocked on the door and told them, 'Guess you don't know me, but my name is Silas Findley.' And that's where I got the nickname.

"So all my life I've been acting. Couldn't preach. Couldn't commit myself to that be-

cause it would have been hypocritical—so much I couldn't believe. Acting was the only thing that really interested me, and it was the antithesis of preaching to my family. To my mother it was everything that was sinful, and the whole family thought it was terrible when I decided to do some local acting. My folks didn't take my being in *Horn in the West* all that well—my being around all those half-naked women."

Ned married pretty Roberta Jones, daughter of a South Carolina minister. She acted in the show, sang ballads, and meshed in a contagious, happy way with the people around Winkler's Creek. She was known as Bobbi, and neighbors were pleased Ned had found her.

Bolstered by his summer performances in *Horn in the West*, Ned decided in the fall of 1954 to go back to New York to try big-city theater again. Soon, however, he found that he could not get free of the subliminal doubts formed on the Winkler's Creek farm. At auditions he would run a fever.

He and Bobbi began to think of rearing a family. They decided to move to Denver to be in the high mountains again—and also to be near libraries and concert halls and theaters. The Rocky Mountains seemed the proper place to expand life, to begin a family, to seek a fortune.

Ned and Bobbi were young and brave; it did not matter that at first they teetered in their ambitions. In Denver, Ned found work as a television kiddy host. He also opened a barbershop and bought and managed rental property. In his spare time he appeared in community-theater productions.

But difficulties would arise. As the decade of the sixties came on, kiddy shows began to dwindle. The Beatles became the rage; their long hair changed male fashions, and the business of barbering began to lose ground. After twenty-one years in Denver, Ned and Bobbi picked up and moved to California. In West Hollywood they bought a rental business and did well.

"Maybe I can't call it a mistake," says Ned, "but it engendered a lot I'd like to forget. We didn't like Los Angeles, didn't like Hollywood. Although we lived out in Granada Hills, a nice section, it was just a living nightmare to try to bring up children there."

So the Austins sold out again and came back to Watauga County. Now, on King Street in Boone, Ned sometimes barbers, but if he wants to rest or play he leaves the apron on his chair and goes back to Winkler's Creek.

"The old conflict between family and stage is long past," he says.

Ned Austin adored his mother, who was old even when he was a child. Although she came from a family of clergymen, she labored on the farm and married young. The rest of her productive life went to rearing six children and taking care of a hardworking husband.

When Ned was in Colorado a Christmas card came one year. After the printed holiday message, a labored and shaky hand had affixed a signature. It was from a person Ned had never known to read or write.

"Mother," it was signed.

Within the last century, on the same stretch of farmland where Kai Jurgensen found Ned plowing the mountainside that June day in 1954, Ned's grandparents reared their children in a one-room log cabin. After the grandfather's first wife died his work hours lengthened. Now besides tending the farm he had to take care of the children.

One day a Dutch-German widow came to the farm. She introduced herself, and the grandfather knew from the meeting that the widow was one who stood against cruel winds.

She told the grandfather that she understood he had seed corn and that she wished to buy some.

For long moments he looked at her in silence. Then he said, "Yes, ma'am, I do have some seed corn. But I'm not going to sell you any."

The woman was stunned. "You aren't?"

"No," he said finally, "I'm going to marry you."

Two weeks later Grandfather Austin drove his mule and wagon to the widow's cabin, picked up her meager belongings, and brought them to his own place.

Although both the grandfather and the widow had children of their own, they would in time add six more. The oldest was Samuel Austin, who inherited part of the land, where he farmed and operated a sawmill. Samuel married the preacher's daughter, and they reared six children—Ned the youngest. Samuel built a big house, and his sons helped with the crop.

Ned remembers that life was never easy, but the Austins did not lack basic necessities.

"In the land of Winkler's Creek," says Ned, "we supported each other. When Uncle George's house burned down, Daddy turned his sawmill to a family advantage; he prepared the lumber, and neighbors came in and helped; the house was put up in two weeks."

People of the valley could do many manual tasks. An "unhandy" family could not possibly live as well as those who built and devised for themselves, but Ned thinks that everyone tried to be self-reliant and not borrow heavily.

"When I was a child," he says, "we never said, 'Yes, sir,' 'No, sir,' 'Yes, ma'am,' 'No, ma'am.' That's because children were just as important to the welfare of the family as adults were. We all worked. Everybody had to go out and hoe corn; everybody had to do whatever was to be done."

There was, Ned contends, more mutual respect between adults and children than could be found in other social climates. "There's something to be said for that. We learned to make do with whatever we had. Like when you go to Mexico, you'll find some of the finest mechanics. That's because they have to make do and they have to figure out how to do it."

One day a man from South Carolina arrived in the community. He brought twelve black men, rented many acres of farmland, and planted tomatoes. The Austins could not understand why the man would want to grow tomatoes in the mountains when the soil and climate were excellent where he came from.

They reasoned that was why the man did not return the next year. He left Winkler's Creek in the fall with eleven black men; the twelfth, named Rob, stayed behind and moved in with the Austins; he shared a room with Ned. Soon Rob married a young woman from Boone, and they set up housekeeping in an old dwelling on Sam Austin's farm.

When a severe blizzard came Rob found he had not laid in enough wood for fuel, and his wife and first child were cold. Just as neighbors had got together to build Uncle George Austin's house, they again pitched in; they brought wood from the forests and chopped enough to keep Rob and his family warm well into the spring.

"I used to want to get as far away from Winkler's Creek as I could," says Ned. "That's why later I could so easily empathize with black people and their struggle. I used to go to Charlotte with my big brother. I was just a little fellow, but I helped him haul produce. I knew that the workers at the distributor's warehouse down there were laughing at us. We were hillbillies, you know; but they were as much hicks as we were; yet they wanted somebody to look down on. So I always felt for black people, being pushed down to a lower class."

Their children now gone, Ned and Bobbi live in the old homeplace, a large white farmhouse built by Ned's father; it sits within sight of where the Austin grandfather bought and homesteaded the three thousand acres he eventually was to own.

Ned and Bobbi have long given up playacting, but now they can rock on the porch of their rambling Winkler's Creek home and talk about their days on stage and the love of drama they handed down to their heirs.

A son, Sam, named for his grandfather, is imbued with his parents' love of the stage. One day not long ago Sam called home and hinted that his mother should buy a new dress. She would need it, he said, when she came to New York to see a production he had cowritten. The show would mark the grand opening of a Waldorf-Astoria restaurant, and Sam would narrate it.

A daughter, Genevieve, has played in New York cabarets, and another son, Robin, regularly performs in community theaters. Robin's sons, Grant and Jordan, both in high school, act in the same theaters, as does their eight-year-old sister, Noelle.

When Noelle was four she played Tinker Bell in a *Peter Pan* drama at Appalachian State University. Ned watched as his tiny granddaughter flitted across the stage on a wire. The cheers took him back to a time when he, too, had performed before an Appalachian State audience. The applause for Noelle seemed the same as that long-ago evening when Ned played Tom Thumb. That was the night playacting first took hold of him.

Food Canner

LIBBY PRITCHARD JOHNSON

EVERY LATE SUMMER it is like this. For two weeks, more or less, Libby Pritchard Johnson works in a steamy kitchen putting up the yield of her garden in quart-size Kerr and Mason jars. She does this even though the cellar—her can room—is bountifully stocked with fruits and vegetables preserved as far back as four and five summers ago.

It is not that Libby must lay in supplies of canned goods to make ends meet or to survive the winter. She has an income from her cleaning service, and her husband, Larry, is an independent electrician; together they have modest resources, and their expenses are sparing. The hard winters are no threat to their sustenance. Still, Libby Johnson is driven year after year to replenish the food she took from her cellar the previous winter. To manage surplus she takes down the oldest preserves first; the current product will be eaten four and five years from now. One might wonder why she does not take a hiatus one summer to reduce the inventory. But such a notion is unthinkable.

Canning is in her blood; she has an addiction to hot and difficult work, an August ritual she has delighted in for as long as she can recall. She remembers herself as a toddler in her grandmother's kitchen; she thinks upon her days as a schoolgirl bearing vegetables from the

Libby Johnson and daughter Alison, Pineola, North Carolina

garden and fruit from the orchard; she recalls her mother's kitchen techniques, her ways of canning, a visceral and necessary task of life. To her, August has never been a time for vacations. Indelibly it is the month when one stands over a cookstove and lays away the gifts of summer—for family, for visiting kinfolk, for church friends, for the clergy and their families.

Libby is cheerfully voluble on the subject of canning: "It's hard work, but it's my thing. I like to go down in the wintertime to see what I've done back in the summer. I can go back this afternoon—go just by myself—and look over what I did two years ago, five years ago. Quiet and private. There's a lot of work that's done that goes down a production line, and the person who creates it never sees it again. I like to see what I've done. Like to recall the summers."

Canning is not an art she consciously cultivated. It is as much a part of her as the quickness of speech, the fetish for cleanliness, the inquiring mind. She is the daughter and granddaughter of mountain clergymen—eloquent and persuasive men, well versed in the Holy Bible, whose wives zealously supported their efforts and kept their homes spotless and their gardens free of weeds. Libby, the only girl and the eldest of five children, preserved a strong feminine independence while tightly bonding with her puritan elders, who were God-fearing paragons she would forever admire.

In early life her father's parents were to her an inseparable part of the family: "They were among the most stable things in my childhood, as much in my life as my own parents. To me they were perfect."

The grandfather, Willard Pritchard, was a man of the gospel. He would set up a church and remain there for a few years before moving on to establish another. Until Libby was thirteen she and her parents lived either in the same house or down the road from Willard and his wife, Emma.

The elder Pritchards were frugal people, and there was real need for Emma to preserve foods. Canning had been essential to her forebears. For Emma it was a solemn rite that she would never dream of shirking.

To supplement his income Willard Pritchard built a small grocery store beside his house; it was a convenience for neighbors and a workplace he could manage while writing and studying sermons. When at last he decided to quit the store Emma took over the little building for her own use. The grocery shelving accommodated the thousands of jars of preserved foods which each year before had overflowed her pantry.

Libby laughs to recall the times: "Nobody came to her house without my grandmother cooking for them. If you came and didn't sit down to eat she'd consider it an insult. The old people were like that. She'd go into the kitchen and put on her apron—she always wore a fresh apron—and from the can house she'd prepare a dinner, making many dishes and fresh breads from scratch. She always sent visitors back home with jars of maybe blackberries or rhubarb or jellies. And she was real clean with her cooking, real particular."

As the vegetables grew, Libby and the other children would go into the grandmother's garden and help weed. At harvest, Edith, a favorite aunt, would come over to help, and she and the children would pick beans and put them into tall wooden crates. They would carry the brimming crates into the front yard, and for the rest of the day, under the shade of the great chinaberry tree, they would break beans, to be carried into Emma Pritchard's kitchen for canning.

Through her twelfth year Libby's life was simple and idyllic. Her father, Herbert, followed his own father's footsteps and became a man of the cloth. His income was modest, but Herbert's family was happy enough. The minister to a church in Blowing Rock, Herbert earned additional money by tuning and repairing pianos. But his family was growing, and gradually he became receptive to the idea of a better position. In the early sixties an offer arrived that would turn their lives about.

From Idaho there came a "call" for Herbert to take another ministry. He would be pastor of a church in the town of Lewiston; he would also direct youth activities throughout the state. At first the family did not know about Lewiston or even much about Idaho. But soon Libby and her brothers were to learn that Lewiston, on the Snake River, was so named for the explorer Meriwether Lewis, and that across the river was Clarkston, Washington, named for Lewis's partner, William Clark. Libby was told she would attend Sacajawea Junior High School, named for the Indian woman who interpreted for Lewis and Clark and helped guide them through the Northwest.

A better life was promised. Herbert was told that a parsonage was under construction and that the Pritchards could move into it when it was finished. In the interim they would live in the furnished basement of the church.

It was then that the Pritchards sold, gave away, or junked nearly all their possessions—bedroom suites, sofas, chairs, tables, and Libby's beloved piano. They packed their remaining goods into a trailer for a trip that Herbert reckoned would take a week.

This was no routine decision. Herbert and his family prayed. Their world had always revolved upon the goodness and gentleness of the elder Pritchards. Now they were leaving the family and embarking on a venture into a strange land across the continent.

When Herbert and his family were ready to depart, church friends and relatives gathered in Willard and Emma's ample yard for dinner. They shook hands and hugged the departing Pritchards; they expressed heartfelt wishes for their happiness. Some cried, because never before had they bade goodbye to a family so close but soon to be so far away.

Before leaving North Carolina, Herbert gathered his brood together. He said that they were moving far away, and that the sickness or death of a dear one could take place back in the mountains. He warned that if such a thing should occur there would not be enough money to fly all the family back home: "We cannot afford the cost, but there is always a possibility that such a bad thing will happen."

On that warm August day the family of seven packed into Herbert's little Plymouth Valiant and set off westward. The car had no air conditioning, but even without it the engine labored under the load of passengers and the full trailer behind.

On the way Libby turned thirteen. The seven days in transit were stifling, and the children bickered. Each day the family set out in the morning darkness so as to avoid the heat; before sunrise the entourage sometimes completed a hundred miles. Yet by eleven o'clock the inside of the Valiant became insufferable. After traveling twelve or fourteen hours the family would stop at a motel; this for the children was a daily healing. They stretched their legs and played on the grounds; then, after taking their baths, they retired early.

For Libby the trip left memories: "I saw the arches on the river in St. Louis, and I searched every street as we passed through, looking for a boyfriend I knew in summer camp who now lived there. I was a kid, and I just knew I was going to see Skip out there."

Crossing the Rocky Mountains, the girl and her brothers were awed and frightened. On hairpin curves she peered into chasms that seemed as deep as her North Carolina mountains were tall; she then looked up and realized that the peaks soared just as high as the valleys ran low.

"Most times I was afraid to look down; I thought if we rolled off we'd die. No way out. And it seemed it took forever to get through those mountains. But it was, oh, so beautiful—such tall trees, the cliffs, the colors that changed right before your eyes."

In Lewiston the Pritchards settled in the basement of their church. The rooms were all below the ground and had small scoop windows snug against the ceiling. There was a bedroom for the parents, one for the four boys, and one for Libby—actually a room entirely to herself for the first time. But her new privacy did little to assuage her discontent.

"It was pitiful. I hated it. We had old iron beds, single light bulbs that hung from a cord, and bare concrete floors. Every night my mama cried."

Nor did the prospect of a new parsonage bolster them. Soon they were to discover that the promised home had been "under construction" for fifteen years; the only evidence, however, was a hole in the ground where stagnant water now stood.

Herbert's income was less than anticipated, and the Pritchards did not eat nearly so well as they had back in the North Carolina mountains. Sensing their problems, Grandmother Pritchard began to write often, as much as every day; once a week she enclosed ten dollars, a goodly sum in those times. With those gifts Herbert's family bought groceries.

At Sacajawea Junior High School, Libby often fought back tears. Her peers were distant and standoffish, so unlike the warm, supportive friends she had known back home. For the first time she realized her culture was different, her clothes simple, her Southern mountain accent strange. She tried to talk in such a way that she would be invisible, no different from her classmates. But her tongue formed sounds that had been fixed in her mind long before, the gentle voice of Appalachia. Finally she told herself she was what she was. And she was glad.

Soon she discovered the luxury in being different; she became known in the school; when a teacher asked for volunteers to read aloud, classmates would point to the mountain girl and say, "Let Libby read."

After a year of living in the church basement the family mustered the means to return to North Carolina. Libby and the boys were euphoric. The miseries of going west in the Valiant were by now a bad dream. On the return trip east they scarcely noticed discomforts; in memory, the tedium of it all was erased by the grandeur of the great West.

Today thoughts of that return trip stand out vividly: "The moose along the Wyoming highways with their big old antlers. Some of them down in the rivers with only their heads above water. And the bison, mean and ugly. Huge. Their shoulders so big, and their heads real large. Herds of them, maybe fifty to a herd. But I remember best the antelopes. They were beautiful and stately and elegant, the way they ran in sync, jumped in unison.

"The prettiest land I ever saw, besides our own country, was Kansas. Green. The hills were not like mountains, but high enough that the land wasn't flat. The roads—they'd go on forever."

Back in the mountains, the father moved from pastorate to pastorate, and Libby attended a different school every year. At last the Pritchards moved to Pineola and settled on their ancestral place, which lies just off the Blue Ridge Parkway; it was this locale on which the young girl's thoughts had always centered.

Libby attended high school at Crossnore, and she thrived in her studies. As she had since grammar school, she checked out a book a day from the school library. She especially liked American and English literature, and Greek mythology was a hobby. She played the piano as she always had, and she helped her mother, especially during the canning season.

Libby had been coming to the Pritchard homestead off the parkway as long as she could remember. On her first birthday she was given a puppy, and her father asked what it should be called. "Butchie," the toddler answered.

Butchie, it turned out, was the nickname of a boy a year or so older who visited from next door. Later he was called Butch, and he, Larry Johnson, would grow up to marry the girl Libby.

The wedding of Libby and Larry was a joining of families. The Pritchards and the Johnsons had been friends for more than a half-century. It was natural, then, that Larry's mother should take up where Grandmother Pritchard had left off. She taught the bride what she knew about canning and gardening; she showed by example how to be an efficient tender of a rural home.

Libby credits her love of canning to three persons—her grandmother, her mother, and her mother-in-law. Now she is passing her knowledge to her married daughter, Melissa Pyatte, and to her younger daughter, Alison. She is sure the tradition will survive, that the skills will be carried on by Melissa's daughter, Canaan, well into the twenty-first century.

Next door to Burleson's Garage, in a place called Miller's Gap between Crossnore and Newland, there is a small stone church where Libby Johnson has played the piano for fifteen years. Men of the church went up to Grandfather Mountain and hauled down boulders, which they crushed and laid upon the building's exterior. They built the whole sanctuary.

Such acts are part of being a mountaineer, Libby thinks, part of being a good neighbor. Besides playing the piano she gives the church a tenth of her income and a tenth of everything she cans; she takes the preserves to the church basement, where she places them beside canned goods left by other churchwomen. They are for the use of those in need.

"It's part of a heritage, part of taking care of people. Things happen in life. When someone gets in a bad place someone else has got to be there to help. There are times when you can't help yourself, and that's what mountain people have always done. They help others. That's what the Bible says. Jesus says it, and he knows."

$\mathcal{S}toryteller$

ORVILLE HICKS

IN THE NINETEENTH CENTURY Council Harmon told the old tales. He was known as the source of ancient storytelling. He passed this love to his son Kell, Kell to his daughter Sarah, and Sarah to her shy son Orville Hicks.

A line of yarn spinners that had begun in Europe hundreds of years ago might have ended there had it not been for Orville's older cousin Rosa Harmon, who married Ray Hicks, the six-foot-seven-inch son of dulcimer maker Nathan Hicks.

Ray—who learned the tales and ballads from his Hicks grandparents—would later be recognized as a master of Old World storytelling. He was to become a subject for the British Broadcasting Corporation, *The New Yorker, National Geographic*, and folklore scholars everywhere.

Although Ray and Rosa's children adored the old stories, none would ever captivate audiences in the manner of their father. None would even try. It was Ray who led the launching of a national storytelling festival in Jonesborough, Tennessee's oldest settlement, an hour away from Ray's home on the eastern slope of North Carolina's Beech Mountain.

Besides busying himself as a potato farmer, herb gatherer, wart healer, and shade-tree mechanic, Ray was a back-porch barber. When Orville and his brothers walked over from Valle Mountain on Saturday afternoons Ray would cut their hair and tell them stories.

Orville Hicks, Deep Gap, North Carolina

Listening to grownups was nothing new for Orville and his siblings. Their mother, Sarah, had told them Jack Tales and Grandfather Tales all their lives.

Says Orville, "Daddy'd be gone, working on the WPA—that old government work down toward Morganton—and Mama would tell us a story or two about every evening. We'd go out in the garden, and she'd get a hoe, and she'd sing old ballads; we'd follow behind her doing what we could do; I learned a lot of ballads from her, but I can't carry a tune in a bucket, so I never did sing. We'd all pick beans and peas, and when we come in later we'd sit around breaking the beans and shelling the peas, and she'd tell stories. Maybe some of them she made a little longer to get us to work longer, but we loved it—the only entertainment we had."

Besides working for the WPA, Orville's father, Gold Hicks, was a part-time Missionary Baptist preacher. Although he was admired by family and friends, he was fiercely religious and strict beyond reason. His battery radio was for listening to preachers, gospel singers, and occasional news reports. No other thing.

Electric service came to the mountains of Watauga and Avery Counties in the early fifties, but it was 1964 before Gold Hicks admitted he could afford to have wires brought to his home.

Orville recalls, "We younguns would have a half-hour of lights before he put us to bed. One time the light bill hit three dollars, and Daddy told us that if it ever got that high again he'd have the electricity cut off."

At bedtime Gold and Sarah's eleven children went to their rooms, knelt by their beds, and said their prayers. Their father would then come in, see that they were comfortable for the night, and turn out the light.

"When the light went out the mouth had better go out, too," says Orville. "He'd tell you to shut up one time; the next time, covers would come down, and he'd lay a stick on you."

Television did not exist in Orville's home, and even books were limited: "If what you were reading wasn't the Bible or a schoolbook you'd better not bring it home. Now I'd bring home something like *Little House on the Prairie*, but that was a schoolbook, and we could read things like that.

"Strict as he was, though, we all loved him; he'd give you the shirt off his back."

In the austere bosom of Gold and Sarah Hicks's home there was nonetheless a deep kindness that comes through today in Orville's manner. Perhaps it was passed from both sides of the family. According to Orville, "People said if everybody was like my mother's brothers and my daddy, we'd have a good world."

Such, too, was the atmosphere that molded young Orville's love of telling stories, a passion that conquered an extreme shyness. He looked forward to seeing his cousins, and when Ray and Rosa Hicks brought their boys on visits Orville and his brothers were ecstatic. Ray Hicks told stories (not always to the liking of Gold the father), and young Ted and Leonard Hicks smuggled comic books to Orville.

"We'd sneak around to that back room,

the boys' room, where we'd hide the funny books under the bed so Daddy wouldn't see them. Later, when Daddy wasn't there, we'd read the books. When Ted and Leonard came again we'd swap the old ones back and forth."

With so many ballads and stories in his head Orville found it hard to keep them to himself. Bashful though he was, he felt comfortable with Ray, who would listen to his narratives. Then Orville began to make up stories. He would improvise Jack Tales and conjure completely new yarns. Ray, the old storyteller, would listen in patronal delight.

"Gah, you're good," Ray told him. "Anybody who can make up things like that ought to get started telling the stories like I do."

"No," Orville replied. "I'm too shy. Can't tell stories to nobody but you and Rosa."

But then a schoolteacher from Statesville, a lover of mountain ballads and stories, made one of her frequent visits to Ray and Rosa's home. She learned of Orville and how the boy should be encouraged to tell stories. The woman wanted to meet the young man, to hear his tales. But when she and Ray drove over to Gold Hicks's house Orville saw them coming. He ran and hid in the woods.

On her next visit she drove into Orville's yard and took him by surprise as he lounged on the porch. She coaxed him to tell a story.

One story led to another, and finally Orville's confidence bloomed. Later, when Ray took him over to a Beech Mountain storytelling festival, he spoke for the first time before a large audience.

It is noon on a Tuesday in June, one of Orville's days off from work at the recycling site on Blowing Rock Road. Benny Harmon, his mother's brother's son, sits with him and a friend. They munch ham sandwiches and drink from twelve-ounce Dr. Pepper bottles. They talk of old times. Benny recalls that his father, Addie, and Orville's mother, Sarah, would sit on the porch and tell ghost stories.

Orville: "Seems like life was more easier back then."

Benny: "No television or nothing. Her [Sarah] and Daddy used to tell tales. We'd go up there and visit. Sit on the porch and listen to them. We liked the ghost stories most. It was dark out there, and them telling them scary tales."

Orville: "Like that old road. Called Tough Road. That haunted road above there. They'd tell tales about that road. They was true. I never knowed Mama to tell a lie. She knowed the Bible as good as Daddy did."

Benny: "See, people could hear the wagons a-coming through there, but they couldn't see them. Just a sound like covered wagons coming along that old, rocky road. The old road is still there."

Orville: "Your daddy told us about riding through there of a night on a horse. Something jumped on behind and grabbed him around the waist. He looked over his shoulder, and there was nothing, just something holding him tight. He rode faster. Tried to get out of there. He got to a creek, and the horse jumped it. When he did, the thing let go. They would say, you know, that a ghost won't cross water."

Benny: "And when he got over to the other side everything was just clear."

Orville: "It really happened."

Benny: "Daddy said he'd felt his hair stand up and his hat raise off his head."

Orville: "They said what made the road haunted was that they built it on Sunday, on the Lord's day."

Orville hated school. He preferred to stay on the farm, where his parents raised their own food and had a horse, a cow, and chickens; they did not grow tobacco because Gold, the puritan father, did not approve of smoking or chewing. The farm had all anyone needed; there was always food. In the summer there were fresh fruits and vegetables, and in the fall Sarah would "put up" two to three thousand jars of apples, peaches, beans, squash, blackberries, dew-

berries, wild strawberries, corn, turnips, beets—whatever came from the garden that she had cultivated the summer long.

Except in bad weather Orville stayed away from the classroom. He roamed the woods, where he swung on vines, fished the streams, and told ghost stories to any friend who might be his momentary accomplice. For days on end he stayed away; he told the teacher he had to help his father on the farm, an acceptable excuse of the time. Deep in the forests he knew so well, he built a shack of scrap lumber. He sneaked onto his family's farm and into the smokehouse, where he cut bits off hanging hams; he smuggled the meat back to his lair and cooked it over an open flame. Once Gold discovered a ham that looked suspiciously chewed upon; he threw away the whole ham, puzzled as to what kind of varmint had invaded his smokehouse.

Orville exulted in his illicit freedom and went to school only when bad weather kept him from the forest. On such days he would not be expected to work on the farm, so he felt it prudent to attend class. Once he took home a report card with forty-two failing marks; he earnestly but gleefully told his father that *F* stood for *Fair*.

Yet his days in the woods were numbered. An older brother moved back to Valle Mountain and installed a telephone. After a string of Orville's absences the brother received a call from the principal, who wanted to know where he might locate Orville Hicks.

"He's in school," said the brother.

"No, he's been out for weeks," said the principal.

"Oh, I see," said the brother.

That afternoon Orville did as always. From his place in the woods he heard the school bus coming, and then he began his usual walk home, books under his arm.

"Where have you been?" his father demanded.

"At school," said an offended Orville.

"No, you ain't."

With that, the father took Orville to the woodshed. "Whipped me good," says Orville. "From then on I almost never hid out again."

The Old Testament guided Gold Hicks's life. He could not—nor did he wish to—drive a car. He and his family would walk to Cool Springs Church, where he often preached. He viewed dancing, cards, television, tobacco, and strong drink as iniquitous; he did not brook any such foolishness in his home.

Once, when an older Hicks son drove up from his Siler City home, Gold decided to treat a few of his hardworking boys and girls to a rare delicacy, a cold "sody pop."

Their father sat in front, and the children piled into the back of their brother's car. As they approached a country store eight-year-old Orville spotted a sign: "Drink Good Ole Mountain Dew."

When Gold asked them to choose their drink they all said they would like a cola. Except Orville. He would try the sody pop he'd seen on the sign.

"I'll take a good ole Mountain Dew."

Gold turned instantly from the drink box and rushed out of the store.

"They's a tree out there," Orville recalls, "and Daddy went out and jerked a limb off. Gave me a whipping right there. Told me, said, 'Orville, don't you ever mention moonshine around your daddy again.'"

When a teacher gave Orville a checkers set Gold demanded the boy return it with thanks.

But often on Saturday nights Gold would turn on the radio so the children could hear the Grand Ole Opry on clear-channel station WSM in Nashville.

"He was strict," says Orville. "But we loved him, and he loved us. He'd sometimes do good things for us that I don't think I'd even do for my kids. Like the times with the haystack.

"It was round, tapped out up top with a big, old pole up the middle, maybe ten or twelve feet high. We'd climb up there and hold onto the pole, and when the others would try to get up there we'd kick 'em, beat 'em up. When somebody pulled you off they could take your place. Called it 'King of the Haystack.'

"Well, Daddy came out one evening and looked at them haystacks. He'd worked so hard stacking the hay. But he knew how much fun we were having. And he asked Mama what he ought to do. She told him to build another haystack and let us play on the old one. That way we'd have to keep the hay built up on it, because when we played on it the stack got to looking pretty bad."

Orville says boys and girls of his time played games that would "bore the daylights out of young people today." He mentions television, video games, and computers as things that outmatch any pastime of the country youth of the midcentury.

"Like when Benny'n me played games with cars coming around the Big S, up there on Valle Mountain.

"See, we'd hitchhike. Except sometimes we'd not be going anywhere. Just thumbed rides.

"One time we'd been working and had made a dollar apiece and was a-feeling good. We got up there on the Big S—that's a road that's shaped like an S and winds around the mountain—and me'n Benny stuck our thumb out. A driver looked at us but kept a-going. So me'n Benny took off through the woods and made a shortcut, so that when the man got on around the curve we's standing there with our thumbs out again. The man stopped this time. Said he'd passed two boys that looked something like us, but he didn't pick them up. Well, when we got out, we laughed about it and thought we'd do that again sometime.

"Then one day we hitchhiked another fellow three times."

Orville was in his thirties before he began to be noticed as a storyteller. Ray Hicks, continuing to be his champion, took him along to appear at the Beech Mountain festival. There, Jack Tales and Grandfather Tales were told in the afternoon, but ghost stories were most effective in the dark. That is how Orville got his start.

"Nobody couldn't see me much," Orville recalls, "and that helped a lot."

His confidence increased as he continued to appear before crowds—not only in the North Carolina mountains but throughout the Southeast. The governor of Kentucky made him an honorary colonel, and calls came so often to his home that his wife, Sylvia, had to begin taking his appointments. Orville had met Sylvia Huffman at church when he visited a brother down at Lenoir; they now have four sons, but only one whom Orville feels might possibly succeed him.

Although Jack Tales continue to be his basic fare Orville also tells contemporary stories, some created for the occasion. He thinks that movies and television have heightened interest in live storytelling. Children want to touch his beard; they tell him they wish they could be Jack; and both they and their parents have him autograph their programs.

Friends encouraged Orville, but Gold Hicks was skeptical. "Orville," he said ruefully, "I've always tried to tell people the truth, and you're out there telling them lies."

Gold Hicks died in 1994. For weeks he lingered ill in the hospital at Banner Elk, occasionally visiting other patients before he became totally bedridden.

Once, shuffling through the corridor, he came upon doctors and nurses taking their seats in a large room.

"What are they doing?" he asked.

"Getting ready for a meeting, Reverend Hicks."

To the old Missionary Baptist there was only one kind of meeting—a prayer meeting. So he made his way into the room and announced he wanted to take part. As the speechless group looked on, Gold Hicks sang his favorite hymn, "Amazing Grace." Somewhat in awe, the staff members murmured thanks, and Gold raised his cane po-litely as he exited. Wanly the group waved back.

His condition worsened in the weeks that followed; at last he sent for his children. As Gold awaited death his offspring came, some singly, some in pairs. They grasped his hand and prayed with him. A daughter, holding back tears, sang "Amazing Grace." When Orville arrived Gold pointed to the Holy Bible on his bedside table and said he was prepared to go.

"He told me he loved me and said for me not to worry about where he was going. He said, 'Just worry about where you're going.'"

Orville understands that he lives in two worlds. He thrives in one and yearns for the other.

"With my children and the new generation coming along, I can't live the old ways. Can't even buy a wash pot. We've got a car and a VCR and television, and our children are growing up fine. But if it was up to me I'd take all the electricity out of the house and have oil lamps. Live the old way."

Orville Hicks thinks of himself as coming out of another time. He is not concerned that his love for the old ways will keep him back. He says he does the best with what he has; he works when there is work; he tells stories when he is called upon.

"Yeah, I've been out of work—lost jobs, no paycheck, nothing coming in for weeks. If I need money I'll trade things like Benny does. But something always comes up. My younguns never went hungry. We do all right. I don't worry."

Dulcimer Masters

ELLIS AND JASON WOLFE

THE LAWN RUNS OFF to Dry Hill Road, an erstwhile pathway to Old Butler, which now rests under fathoms of water. If you follow the road you will find no outlets; down the hill, you loop back; after three miles you again pass Ellis Wolfe's house.

Wolfe—lazing in his lawn swing on a warm summer day—is surprised that so many people have yet to learn that the road will not take them to New Butler and beyond. Years ago engineers impounded the Watauga River and filled the valley where the town of Old Butler had thrived. Still, almost every day, people stop to ask, "Will this road take me to Butler?"

Ellis reckons that old notions die hard. Drivers have been asking the same question since his grandfather Columbus grew tired of being doubted. The old man began to give short answers to insistent passersby.

"Where does this road go?" they would ask.

"It don't go nowhere," the grandfather would say.

"Don't it go to Elizabethton?"

"No. You can't go that way."

"Well, where does this road go to?"

Ellis and Jason Wolfe, Dry Hill, Tennessee

"Sonny, it don't go no damn where."

At times a mockingbird in a nearby oak sings; its sound is rich and piercing. Ellis Wolfe pauses. He watches a red sports car thunder down the road in the direction of his grandfather's *no damn where.*

"Has the traffic picked up?" he asks rhetorically.

"Oh, Lord, here just recently it's out of sight," he answers. "You never know who they are. I'd say twenty-some families live down in here, but nine-tenths of the cars that come down this road don't belong in here."

Though Dry Hill Road is but a country highway the road sounds are invasive, discordant with Ellis's own ingrained symphony. Even as he speaks there is the happy timbre of the mockingbird, the distant hum of his son's tractor beyond the meadow's rim, and the steady drone of bees in flight. A sudden engine roar, foreign to the gentle sounds of rural life, interrupts the rhythm of his being. He is a quiet man, and he speaks in rich, low, unhurried tones.

"Now, the road there. We used to go that way to Butler. That is, before it was covered by the lake and before New Butler developed. I went to school in Old Butler, to Watauga Academy. A girl I went to school with introduced me to Cora, my wife. Cora and I went down that road to go buy things, went there to go to Elizabethton. After the dam came we had to go back and around the lake to get to New Butler."

The road goes through Dry Hill, a scattering of farms and homes, shown in fine print on Tennessee maps. It runs along the valley beneath Dry Run Mountain, east of the lake. The area gets its name honestly, because there are no underground reservoirs, or running streams, or even springs or wells. Until conduits were recently laid into Dry Hill, generations of Wolfes subsisted on rainwater collected off their barn roofs into cisterns.

Ellis says that because there are no factories near its shores Watauga Lake is the least-polluted body of water in the country. Yet if he had his way there would be no lake: "I'd rather have it the way it was. Butler was a beautiful little town; it would have been a nice place by now. They took thousands of acres of level farmland, the best land there was in the country. By now we'd have been a suburb of Butler. It would have grown out to here."

Those who lived in the town were moved

five or six miles away and called their transplanted home New Butler, but Ellis thinks the place will never become what Old Butler meant to East Tennessee.

Ellis Wolfe was a grown man and "amazed" when at Blowing Rock, North Carolina, he first heard a dulcimer. Dulcimers were being played all around Beech Mountain, but they were scarce in the Dry Run hills.

Although the sound of the dulcimer drew him it was the idea of crafting the instrument that spurred him. His great-grandfather had come from the Black Forest of Germany, and a tradition of precision craftsmanship had followed the family line through Virginia and into East Tennessee. Ellis's grandfather, a woodworker, and his father, a farmer, worked the same spread of land that Ellis and his son and grandson now live upon. Ellis followed the woodcrafting line naturally; he was often sought for his ability to build stairways. And as a sideline—it was never to be anything else—Ellis built dulcimers in the basement. When fine dust began filtering up into the house he had to move his workshop to a shack behind his home.

Soon Ellis was drawn to dulcimer maker Stanley Hicks. Without seeing each other's work the two had independently created similar patterns for their dulcimers. Long before Stanley died he began referring all inquiries about dulcimers to Ellis.

But walnut dust, having stopped Stanley from making dulcimers, at last halted Ellis Wolfe, too.

Ellis's grandson, Jason, joins him on the lawn. From his home on the hillside above, Jason brings two musical instruments—a dulcimer that Ellis crafted and a fretless banjo that Jason made under Ellis's guidance. The bottom of the dulcimer is carved of what Ellis calls crotch walnut, the sides of bent walnut, the top of wormy butternut wood. This one has a rare look; it does not resemble a rustic dulcimer; rather, it is fitted precisely and finished as handsomely as a fine violin. Because butternut wood is brittle, Ellis says, the tone is better.

Jason tenderly lays the dulcimer and banjo in an empty lawn chair. He intends to play both but first wants to join the conversation. Having been chatting with his grandmother Cora outside the house, he has overheard Ellis talking of Dry Hill Road. Now he wants his grandfather to tell of the old days on the road—of the circuses, the turkeys, the sheep. There is between them an easy and unmistakable respect. Before telling of the old days on the road Ellis introduces Jason, saying that not only can the young man craft a dulcimer, he can play one beautifully.

"Yeah, the circus," he continues. "See, they moved the circus through about every year, and from the railroad station in Butler they'd go to Boone. They couldn't take the elephants up Watauga River because of the high bridges, lots of them. So those old elephants would go flopping up that road. For a fellow growing up out here that was a sight. Odd, you know."

Now his talk of the elephant parade leads Ellis to other memories of the road.

"Flocks of turkeys. They drove them out of North Carolina to load them on the train in Butler. I don't know how they'd do it, but there was a turkey out front, and it had a bell around its neck—a bell-turkey, they called it. There'd be two or three hundred turkeys following right down the road. The drover would be behind them, and they'd put them in a pen at the depot, put them in freight cars, and [be] gone with them. They did cattle and sheep the same way.

"Now the most amazing thing was those sheepdogs. If they were bringing sheep down this road, when the herd got down there to my driveway, why there'd be a dog standing there, keeping those sheep from following any path off the road. Other dogs would go on down there to my great-grandfather's place, and you'd see them standing there. Wouldn't let those sheep get in anybody's gate, anybody's driveway. A drover would be walking along behind them, but those dogs were the ones that were taking the sheep right on."

Ellis looks at the instruments Jason has brought out. He says his own years of making dulcimers with Stanley Hicks encouraged Jason's love of old mountain music. Ellis and Stanley were partners "of sorts," and through their relationship Jason developed a mastery of the dulcimer.

Stanley's heritage of both making and playing dulcimers came from his parents, his grandparents, and generations beyond memory. His father and mother played dulcimers, banjos, and violins. Stanley kept the tradition alive—and in fact heightened it—by making instruments and performing on crude stages throughout the mountains.

He and his wife, Virgie, had only one child, a son who worked hard but never cared to play an instrument or sing or even listen to the old ballads and tunes. So when one day Ellis took Jason across Dry Run and Stone Mountains to Stanley's vine-covered workshop, Stanley took to Jason, who at that time could play barely more than one dulcimer tune—"Amazing Grace," the piece his grandfather had taught him.

"When I learned that song it was in the wintertime," says Jason. "And although Papaw will tell you he can't play, he can. He taught me that song, and I played it for

months, till I got sick of it."

Jason's aunt Vicki, who plays guitar and piano, then taught the boy—who was twelve at the time—to pick out other tunes on the dulcimer. She would write down the notes and designate the fret numbers.

"I got to where I could play a few songs, and Papaw started taking me to Stanley's. That's where I started learning how to play, how to get the rhythm of songs—playing the old-time way."

For Stanley, Jason was a godsend. As the years passed he had grown sensitive to the dwindling number of mountain people who played and sang the old way. He enjoyed his place as a keeper of the ancient musical arts. But in his late seventies, and notable as he was, he had never known anyone to sit at his feet, to want to play music in the way of his mother, his father, his ancestors.

Now there was Jason.

"Stanley would pull up a chair, and we'd sit knee to knee," says Jason. "I could see him play up close, and I could play right with him. He'd play songs just normally, but sometimes he'd slow down for a little bit. We'd go over there about once a week; every time, by the time Papaw was ready to leave, I could play a new song pretty well. Back home, I'd run the song over and over in my mind until I could eventually get it."

Jason lays the dulcimer on his lap. He holds a fret stick in his left hand and a pick carved from a plastic milk bottle in his right; he noodles the strings. His grandfather asks him to play "Turkey in the Straw," and Jason begins, softly at first, then increasing in volume to compete with the mockingbird, which has begun to sing louder. Apparently it takes its cue from the sweet strumming sounds; when the tune ends the bird becomes silent.

"When we'd get to Stanley's house," says Jason, "the first thing he'd tell me was, 'Let's boil a cabbage.' We'd always start out playing that one."

He strums a tune that despite its title— "Boil That Cabbage Down"—is surprisingly lyrical and haunting.

The silvery music draws Cora and a guest from the house, and they stand silently just in back of Jason. The trees sway in a fresh breeze, and the mockingbird flies away. Atop a green pasture that rises nearly a thousand feet behind the house, cows huddle in the shade of oaks and poplars. Jason plays "Red River Valley," and the tune is consonant with the breeze, the cattle on the hill, the serenity of this summer afternoon under Dry Run Mountain.

By fourteen Jason could play well enough that Stanley Hicks and another musician asked him to join their musical performance at Appalachian State University. There, be-

fore an audience of a thousand, Jason played in unison with two of the most noted dulcimer players in the Southern mountains. After the show veteran performers grabbed his hand. One of them told Ellis, "That boy Jason set up there as cool as a cucumber. If I'd went out there at that age somebody'd had to pour me out of my shoes."

Jason played at festivals throughout the mountains—Beech Mountain, the Carter Mansion, Jonesborough Days, Trade Days— and he continued to go back to Stone Mountain every week to play duets with Stanley.

His health failing, Stanley seemed eager to transfer all his knowledge of the old music to his protégé. Jason remembers Stanley as kind and lighthearted: "He'd tell audiences that to get to his place you'd have to ride as far as you could ride, run as far as you could run, walk as far as you could walk, crawl as far as you could crawl, and then you'd come to where he stayed."

In the fall of 1989 Jason and his father visited Stanley, who was home from the hospital. The boy brought his dulcimer but was reluctant to play. Stanley insisted, yet Jason feared that the requests were simply out of courtesy; Stanley seemed to be feeling low. After a few short tunes Jason put away his dulcimer, and he and his grandfather whispered to each other. They feared the end was near. When they started to leave, Stanley called them back. He said Jason must play one other tune—"Sweet Bye and Bye," one of the first tunes he'd taught the boy.

"That seemed to please him," remembers Jason. "We left after that, and I guess that was the last dulcimer tune Stanley ever heard. I think it was his favorite song—the prettiest I had ever heard him play. Within a week or so after we were there Stanley died."

It is Jason Wolfe who represents the continuum of mountain music that began in Stanley Hicks's family two hundred years ago. He does not know how far in the future the tradition will stretch, but he believes he is the only person alive who plays the old man's style. Though he appreciates other music he strongly prefers the rhythm and feel of the ballads Stanley played out of the past.

The Wolfes have worked the same spread in Dry Hill for well more than a century.

Jason needs only lift his eyes from the dulcimer to see the same white house in which his great-great-grandfather Columbus lived. He knows the story—how the old man in his youth was drafted to serve under his brother in the Confederate army but within days deserted and joined the Union. Such were the divided sentiments in East Tennessee. During summers around the farm Columbus refused to wear shoes; because of this crusty and nonconformist nature, the barefooted Columbus lost a big toe while cutting hay with a scythe. His son Lawrence, a studious young man, taught at Watauga Academy.

Young Jason, now a student at East Tennessee State, represents the fifth generation to live on the Wolfe farm. He loves playing dulcimers but is not sure how long he will craft them.

Whatever career lies ahead (he hoped once to be a forest ranger), Jason says he wants to be where it is quiet. "I'll try my best to live in a place like this. Always."

$\mathscr{W}oodcarvers$

ON A MONDAY MORNING in the summer of 1953, fourteen-year-old Baxter Presnell went out to help his father in the cabbage patch. He had not felt well since yesterday's picnic, when a bad headache had sent him home to spend the rest of the day in bed. This morning he thought it unusual that he had not fully recovered. Yet he knew his father, Edd, would need help cutting cabbages. As he worked in the patch his head began to throb harder, and pains on the backside of his neck finally drove the boy inside, where he lay down again.

When Edd came in for the noon meal he thought something curiously wrong; he had never known Baxter to go to bed in the middle of the day. Perhaps a doctor was needed. When he mentioned this to his son, now lost in pain, there was no objection.

At the hospital in Banner Elk, Baxter's malady was diagnosed as poliomyelitis. Watauga County was being hit by a rash of polio that summer, but Baxter's case was unusual in that there were no other infections in the family—none even within miles. Baxter was sent ninety miles south to Asheville, where he joined other victims for many months of treatment.

Another year was to pass before Dr. Jonas Salk introduced a vaccine that would rid the world of polio.

At the hospital in Asheville, Baxter was adrift in an alien world. He appreciated the good medical care, but slowly he came to understand that he would be forever different.

Besides undergoing treatment and rehabilitation, he was occupied with daily tutoring. In his bed he dreamed of the old homeplace at the dead end of Old Mountain Road. He had always been certain he would one day tend the crops in the fields of his mother's parents. But now he was bewildered; strange things had happened to his body. Would he—a strapping youngster who had weighed a hundred pounds at the age of ten—have the strength and agility to manage a farm?

When at last he was released from the hospital Baxter continued to dream of farming. But he was forced in time to yield to reality. Life would never be the same. Today he thinks his physical limitations set him upon a woodcarving career—one that would alter even his father's dulcimer making and eventually the labors of his future wife, Reva.

In the ninth grade Baxter came to grips with the fact he would no longer walk as others did. Still, every school morning, he trudged over a difficult gravel road to wait for the school bus. At last he surrendered; he would no longer attend classes.

For five months after quitting school he was beside himself. He could not attend classes, nor could he do farm work. To occupy his days he whittled figures of people, animals, and birds. This was an offshoot of a crude wintertime craft of his father and his maternal grandfather, John Benjamin Hicks, who occupied themselves by carving bowls, nails, scoops, dough trays, and butter ladles. Country grocers bought some of these utensils for in-store use. His father's dulcimer making fascinated Baxter, but this, he knew, was work too strenuous for his crippled body.

The boy was acquainted with Richard Chase, a folklorist who had come to live near Laurel Creek and who gathered Jack Tales and Grandfather Tales for books he published. Chase saw talent in young Baxter and urged him to start carving seriously. Further, he said he would drive Baxter to Kentucky to visit Berea College.

For those who needed financial help, cash for tuition was unnecessary at Berea. Students worked in shops to earn enough for expenses and classes; their academics included hands-on training. Finally Chase convinced Baxter to try Berea. If it turned out badly the boy was free to return home.

In the first week Baxter would indeed have retreated to Beech Mountain, but there was no transportation. The second week was better; he met new friends and settled in.

*Reva and Baxter Presnell and daughter Rosanna,
Laurel Creek, North Carolina*

He soon learned to make handicrafts by using patterns. His products were sold at craft centers in the town of Berea. The boy earned thirty-five cents an hour, good pay for the times.

One of his woodcraft instructors was a Mr. Smith from Great Britain. Smith's speech was so strange that Baxter thought he was from a land where English was not spoken. He likes to tell the story: "I asked him, 'How long you been speaking English?' Smith said, 'All my life. How long have you been slaughtering it?'"

It was during his first year at Berea that Baxter persuaded his father to begin edging out of farming and into crafts. Edd drove up to Berea with samples of his carvings; there he was encouraged to join a craft guild called the Council of Southern Mountains. This led to Edd's first woodcraft showing the following year in Asheville.

Baxter began to love Berea. He earned his tuition and filled his pockets with money. He and his friends often worked on Saturdays without pay. They were fascinated by their growing skills; they carved leaves and flowers from oak, hickory, poplar, dogwood; all were without patterns and done for the sheer fun of it.

At other times Baxter and his friends would pack food and blankets and camp deep in the forest at the Pigg House, so named for a family who had once lived there. In winter the pipes were shut off, and water for coffee came from a nearby creek.

Once a farmer told them of a cave he thought had never been explored. Despite his physical handicap Baxter went with five friends to probe it. They dropped wood scraps as they crawled through the maze of tunnels. Upon their return they failed to find a key marking and had to worm their way through the labyrinth for hours before emerging exhausted and thirsty, their flashlights "just about dimmed out."

After nearly four years at Berea, Baxter earned a high-school diploma and came back to Watauga County. Then for more than three years he studied industrial arts at Appalachian State, becoming the first on either side of his family ever to attend college. But he "butted heads" with an English professor and didn't complete his degree. "No way I could get out of her class," he says. "I just gave up and quit. I decided I'd just make my way carving wood."

Back home, he worked with his father in a little shack outside the family home. Edd's dulcimer making had already distinguished him. He was now an active member of a craft guild, and he farmed less and created more. He designed, turned, and carved exquisite goblets from elm wood, bowls from rhododendron burl, biscuit cutters from fruit wood. He made furniture and sometimes, as a special favor, even coffins. His handicrafts by and by would nudge him out of farming altogether.

Baxter's mother, Nettie, joined in carving birds and animals. She also played Edd's dulcimers. When pioneer music began sweeping the country in the sixties, sound technicians from Eastern cities made their way to the end of the road to record Nettie's playing. Edd was pleased; after all, the first dulcimer he ever heard had been played by the schoolgirl Nettie, the daughter of Julie and John Benjamin Hicks, who lived in the very place the Presnells now called home.

Their industry began to flourish. In winter the Presnells would build their inventory of carvings, and Edd would catch up on orders for dulcimers; from spring through fall the family would deliver their stock to craft shows in Asheville, Bristol, Abingdon, even as far away as California. For years an old sign near the Banner Elk–Valle Crucis highway pointed northward toward the workshop, and tourists braved the rocky, dusty, often muddy road to the Presnell homeplace.

In time Edd would build a brick house on a little rise north of the spring; Baxter and his new wife, Reva, would occupy the old Hicks homeplace on the opposite knoll. Two work shacks burned, one a few years after the other; the current shack was built little differently from the first two; it is primitive but adequate even in harsh cold, except on days when a northwest wind blows hard. At such times the Presnells take a piece or two of their carvings and return to work in the warmth of their home.

For forty years Edd Presnell was perhaps the best known and most photographed of the Appalachian dulcimer makers. He was slight and wiry, his beard reaching his waist. He worked from dawn to dusk and distinguished himself by making money doing a thing he loved. He was outwardly stern and inwardly gentle.

"Baxter's a whole lot like his daddy," says Reva. "Especially with his patience. Papaw was a patient man, and Baxter's got a lot of that in him, too. I'd hate to have to go through all he's gone through."

Once Edd and a brother of Nettie's were driving to town when Edd's car became bogged in a deep mudhole. Losing no time, Edd jumped out and pulled a set of chains and a shovel from the trunk. He whistled a tune while he mired himself in mud and began digging out.

"How in the world can you whistle in a situation like this?" said Nettie's brother.

"It's just as good to whistle as it is to cry," said Edd.

When Edd and Nettie moved into their brick home, Baxter and his new wife settled down less than a hundred yards away in the two-story dwelling where Nettie had lived since birth. In his spare time Edd continued to improve the joint property. He cleared the area with a dragline and used a bulldozer to dam the water from a free-flowing spring between the houses, making a small pond. From the overflow he built a larger pond below, in an area that had been swampy and gorged with pine stumps and briar bushes. In the ponds he stocked bass and bream, and soon frogs found homes there. Along the paths around the ponds now grow lush ferns, huckleberry bushes, and healthy hardwood trees. They form a background for the broad greensward that Edd planted and groomed. It was here that son Baxter and a friend decided one summer to have a party of friends.

"We called it a pig picking," says Baxter. "We bought a suckling pig, put it on a spit, and roasted it over the coals. Had fifteen or twenty people there."

The second year, more people came, and it was then that Edd offered to take over. He would finance the project and have an annual pig picking—one that would accommodate two hundred or more friends. In the years after that he raised hogs to provide meat for the occasion. But one day it became obvious that he did not have enough time to grow, slaughter, dress out, and barbecue pigs for so many guests, so he began to buy meat for an event that drew larger crowds each year.

Reva observed intently as Baxter carved birds, animals, leaves, and figures of people. Although she helped her husband in cutting crude pieces from patterns, she was not confident she could ever become a skilled woodcarver.

"Now Baxter kept telling me I could do it. I kept telling him I couldn't. I'd made little ornaments, but when it got to real carving I thought I couldn't. But he told me if I'd just do it I could sell everything I made."

In time Reva began to take her talent more seriously. Baxter would remind her that she had been a top student in school, that she had dropped out only because she thought life would be better on the farm.

Slowly she gained confidence. She studiously watched Baxter and his mother carve wooden baubles—dogwood pins, flowers, earrings. She was pleased when her products began to sell, astonished that every morning she was itchy to get to work in the little shop. She labored six hours or more every weekday, until her back ached and her hands grew stiff. At craft shows she learned the language and the culture of woodcarving. Gradually it came over her that she had become a professional—a respected one—and that carving would be her life.

In the process she came to realize that she had an unusual liking for wood.

"Wood talks to me," she says. "One day Papaw was making a dulcimer there in the shop. He had cut the body out of the most beautiful cat's-paw maple I'd ever seen. I walked by, and that wood spoke to me. Said, 'Look at me. How pretty I am.' And right then I knew I had to have that dulcimer. That beautiful wood cried out to me."

The dulcimer Edd crafted from the cat's-paw maple was of a special design, one Reva thought fitting for the exquisite wood. There were dogwood inlays, and carved-out hearts for sound holes, and redbirds perched on dogwood limbs. Reva thought the instrument the prettiest she had ever seen.

"I came home and told Baxter. I told him I'd scrimp to get it. So I brought it home, and Papaw let me buy it in payments. He could have sold it for much more, but he saw how much I wanted it, and I believe he was happy for me to get it."

On a Sunday morning in March 1990 Baxter and Reva were at church in the

Rominger settlement when the message reached them. Their house, the ancient home of Baxter's grandparents, was burning.

When they arrived at the scene, volunteer firefighters from Cove Creek and Banner Elk were pumping water from Edd's ponds; they managed to save a bedroom, but the rest of the house and its contents were lost.

"In a sense it was like a death," says Reva. "You lose things that stand for people you love, things they made, their gifts, things that no amount of money could buy. I had a collection of the pieces Baxter made before he got sick. His work now can't be replaced, because his health won't let him carve anymore. And Edd's dulcimer, it's gone—the one with the beautiful wood that talked to me."

Reva and Baxter moved in with Edd and Nettie until their new house could be built. It would face the same direction as the old one. Before the ground was cleared for the new dwelling they combed the ravaged remains. They scratched out a walnut carving, a dulcimer, and a few still-useful household items. They found some of the gifts they cherished, among them gewgaws and craft-show items that reminded Reva of those who had given them.

"There was one [craftsperson]. I don't remember her name now, and I probably couldn't speak it anyway—a little German lady, one of the sweetest people you ever met in your life. She made little angels. When I met her, well, me'n her took to each other right at once. She'd take me around and introduce me to people. And she gave me a little treetop angel and wouldn't take money for it. I used it on our Christmas tree every year. It went up in smoke. The lady's dead now, but I still got my memory of her and the angel that was a piece of her."

In July 1994 more than two hundred visitors from the South, East, and even the Far West lined their cars along the dead end of Old Mountain Road. They brought dulcimers Edd Presnell had made over many years. They laid them out on long tables, and Papaw talked with them; he signed pictures and books and magazines. Having mailed most of the instruments, he had not before met most of the owners.

The visitors brought covered dishes, and at noon Reva helped spread plates of roast pig. After picnicking on the greensward and around the ponds, Edd's offspring awarded prizes for the oldest, the youngest, and the farthest-traveled guest. The prizes were elegant wooden goblets Edd had turned by hand.

It was, Baxter thinks, probably the best day of Edd's life. The event had been planned in February, and even up to the time of the Dulcimer Homecoming no one knew that Papaw was sick. Within two weeks Edd Presnell was dead.

The following year Baxter and Reva were hosts to another pig picking, honoring Edd's last-day wish that the event continue. They saw new faces that year, but it was not possible for the younger Presnells to meet all of the milling visitors.

Nettie, Edd's widow, clear-eyed and brightly dressed, sat in her wheelchair and greeted everyone who came near. She grasped hands, and she hugged friends and kinfolk.

Cabinet Craftsman

BILL CORNETT

BILL CORNETT'S FATHER was born in the hills of Virginia. When he was very young he was taken to Kentucky, where he lived until he was grown. Then he ranged southward to North Carolina, where he settled in the locus of his ancestors—the meadows and mountains of Bethel. It was here, snug in a verdant valley of the Watauga River not far from the eastern edge of Tennessee, that he married and settled down. Bill, one of his sons, was born and reared here. To them both, the land would always be magical.

Bill's father and mother reared five sons and four daughters. They raised potatoes and corn and grew hogs that they occasionally bartered for sugar and coffee. They tended a patch of tobacco but earned most of their income by running a sawmill. For three years Bill's father commuted daily to Grandfather Mountain, twenty miles distant; there he did backbreaking work on timber-cutting crews. He persevered because the pay was better than he could earn on the farm.

The father's task did not do justice to his subtle skills. Hidden under his lumberjack's roughness was a sensitive carpenter—a dedicated and hard-to-please worker in wood. It was only later that he could afford to spend time building a trade from his aesthetic talent.

The home in which the son Bill was born is now gone. Bill spent most of his young life

Bill Cornett, Stone Mountain, North Carolina

within five miles of it. When he grew up he ranged as far as Ohio, where for two years he worked with a brother. He yearned for North Carolina, and one day he packed his clothes and came back to the mountains. For a year he made cabinets in a factory. Then he moved to rural Cove Creek on the Watauga River. Soon he would move again, at last homesteading in a thicket on the slopes of Stone Mountain. There he lived just a few bumpy curves away from instrument maker and musician Stanley Hicks.

He began his career in house carpentry and soon learned to follow his father's ad-

vice: "If you ain't going to do your best, don't even start."

Tall, athletic, and often smiling, Bill moves about his clean and organized cabinet workshop surely, deliberately, his mind focused on the pure joy of doing a thing right.

He was working for an acquaintance in the house-building business when he decided to convert a large shack—a "rough old place"—into a spotless workshop. There he could begin a business without leaving home.

"When I left house carpentry and started this business I thought, 'Well, I don't know if I'll get one single call or not.' This old building was just a pile of junk, but I thought I'd just start right here. Then if I could get work I'd do something to the shop. And you know, in all that time, I've never had the time. Never caught up. So I don't know when I will—next year maybe."

The workshop, less than a hundred steps from his house, sits within a hemlock grove and is visible from the primitive Hattie Hill Road through trees and shrubs. It is quiet. The only noises other than nature's come from Bill's own shop and occasionally from the groan of a vehicle along the dirt road. The floors are clean, the workbenches free of clutter and sawdust. In summer the wide doors are open so Bill can look out upon the trees and hear the bluebirds. He normally works from eight in the morning until seven, sometimes ten, in the evening. No matter the impatience of customers or the backlog of work, Bill will not be hurried.

"I'll lose a job before I'll do that. If I can't suit myself—can't make myself feel good about what I'm making—I won't take the job at all."

As a craftsman Bill is regarded with envy. His business comes from friends and past employers. With his shop far from commercial traffic, and with his sunup-to-sundown work habits, he has had little opportunity to develop business.

"People just call me. I never ask where they heard of me. I guess it's just word of mouth that keeps me behind all the time. People will ask for something, and I'll say, 'Well, I can work it in,' not having an idea how I'll do that. But one way or the other I will, I'll work it in. Sometimes, though, I get more than I really should take."

He employs nobody. His son comes over sometimes to help with the heavy lifting, and a small granddaughter plays around the shop "helping" with things. "She'll use about a bottle of glue a day," says Bill. He likes the company. "If she wants to pick up an electric drill and fool around with it, as long as I think she's not going to get hurt, I don't worry about her. She's careful; won't do her any harm."

He bears his granddaughter's playtime the same kindly way he tolerates all else in his private world. He is intensely creative but handles the pressures of his life calmly; he can take distractions.

"I like it the way I do it now," he says. "I have to work longer hours and probably don't make as much money as I could if I got out and hunted me a job. But I like it this way. Do what I want to. No deadline on how much time I can spend on something to get it like I want it. I like that part."

There are those who search always for meaning in their lives, who suffer the stress of the production of art. Bill Cornett is not among them. His father was a carpenter; his grandfather crafted in wood; his brothers and a son work in the building trades. Life for Bill is simple, perhaps hard at times, but he thinks the rewards come in the way artisans perform their chosen work.

Bill's grandfather Roby had a woodworking shop at nearby Mountaindale, on Pickbritches Creek. The rushing stream powered a waterwheel, which transferred the force into the workshop by way of a revolving shaft; all the tools moved together even if some were not used. The great flood of 1940 washed out bridges and took away homes and buildings. It swept away the grandfather's waterwheel, shop, and tools. He never rebuilt the place because he knew electricity would soon come to the hills, relegating water-powered workshops to the status of oxen and mules.

Roby Cornett and his brother Jim made furniture, ax handles, hoe handles, and peavey handles. People would come and tell the Cornetts they wanted a farm implement or a piece of furniture. Sometimes customers would barter, but when the harvest was good they usually paid cash. It was a local business; the Cornetts did not ship their goods outside the county.

As he grew up Bill sometimes pondered the future. At last he began to tell himself that whatever was good for his grandfather

was good for him. He was not yet born when the 1940 flood came, but he knew the history and realized the reputation his grandfather had gained before the waterwheel and shop washed away. His father reinforced the heritage; excellent work was expected of the Cornetts. Farmers came to them because they wanted carefully crafted products; they knew that when they traded their farm stuffs and paid hard-earned money they would get a dependable product; when on rare occasions there was a problem, they knew the Cornetts would repair or replace a product with no questions asked.

Today Bill Cornett carries on with unusual grace and poise. He says he is fortunate to have the talent of his forebears. He was restless and dissatisfied in the days he worked on construction jobs in Ohio and in the furniture factory, where he labored under someone else's schedule.

"I didn't like it too good. Just had so much time to do something, whether you did it right or did it wrong. I know that to make a profit a factory has to get things out in a reasonable time, but I didn't like that. If it takes fifteen minutes more to do it right I think you ought to go ahead and finish it. Almost anybody will agree to that."

Today, when someone comes in and wants, say, an entertainment center, Bill will figure the time required to turn out a product that will satisfy him. Occasionally the customer will complain, but Bill sticks by his quotations: "I tell them I can't do the work at a lower price if I use the best materials and do the kind of quality that is expected of me. If they want something cheap and in a hurry, something that won't last, I really don't care to have the job."

In the shop are cabinets and other furniture in varying stages of completion. Bill chooses the best grades of wood and crafts the furniture from rough layouts; normally the finished piece is of his own design. After finishing the woodworking he insists on doing the staining or painting himself, because he learned long ago that the best-constructed product can be compromised in the final stage. He does not permit outside carpenters and other workmen to share in any part of the process. He loads the furnishings on his truck, hauls them to the buyers, and installs them in the homes and offices.

"Most of the work I do ends up so that I see the customers again, talk to them again. If they have any problems they tell me. So it's not like, 'Here's the product. Give me the money. I'll never see you again.' I like it when I get to see people, see them living with my work, furniture that could be in their homes the rest of their lives."

Bill thinks his meticulous nature is a family trait: "With his work, my dad was a fussy kind of person—patient, more than anybody I've seen. And my uncle was a real good craftsman, like my grandfather and his brother. I guess whatever I can do, I inherited it. That's the reason I got into it. Never had much of an idea of doing anything else. If I'd ever have done anything else it would have been working in the forest service."

In the mountain woodland where Bill has chosen to stay, he is the envy of visitors. They laugh and say to him that his surroundings are as close to paradise as they expect to come.

"I feel the old-timers who were born and raised here feel the same way. I've heard of mountain people who are a little shy to say their land is beautiful, but I'm not one of them. I love it here. Always proud of it. Good country. Good people. The older ones are getting gone now, but . . ."

There is an aroma of the woods, rich and slightly sweet, a scent different from any ever known in the lowlands. Bill is uncertain how long the purity of his surroundings will last; he wonders if his granddaughter will grow up to live here; he hopes she will be able to protect a precious heritage but fears that preservation will be difficult. He is mindful of all that is taking place even on once-remote Stone Mountain. He sees the first stages of development: surveyors marking off lots, bulldozers tearing out woodlands, signs on trees that tell of property being auctioned to satisfy estates.

"There's one family still up the mountain that I guess you'd call original. Everybody else up here has moved in. The old-timers have died and gone. The old mountain ways are pretty much on the way out."

Cornett seems incapable of speaking ill of others. Like his old-time neighbors, he is tolerant but independent. He says people have a right to do as they please with property that is rightfully theirs, but his indulgence falters when he reflects upon impending changes—violated woods and meadows that will never return to the Edenic state he knew when growing up.

"People my age have probably still got a little bit of mountain in them, but the generation below me, they're totally different from what they used to be."

Bill considers himself a "tweener." He is years younger than was his up-mountain neighbor, the late Stanley Hicks, and decades older than the generation that has lost the ways of the pioneers. He admits that if he could live in any period of history he would go back to the time when each person was an individual—to the time when settlers established their homesteads "without chewing up the wilderness."

When he was young, Bill and his buddies from the Watauga River Valley would pack a flatbed farm truck and drive to Beech Mountain. They would follow a dirt road to the top, to a locale still known as The Pinnacle. There they pitched tents and settled in for the weekend. They locked their food—cornbread, potatoes, raw cabbage, whatever was in season—in lard buckets and cookie tins and stowed it all inside the truck cab to protect it from wild goats.

"I'd love to do that again, but with all the development there, there's no way that could be done."

He still explores the mountains, though not to the extent he did in his youthful days. At times he and his wife will put an old boat into the Watauga River at Guy Ford, a place where pioneers crossed the water with their animals and wagons. From there they float through wild and uninhabited mountains, winding over rocky shoals all the way to Watauga Lake in Tennessee.

They could "throw in" at the ford and reach the lake sooner, but they choose instead to follow the river's meandering course, taking in the wilderness, stopping to stretch and walk on some secluded shore.

Often on Sunday afternoons, with work arranged tidily in his closed shop, Bill and his wife walk in the mountain woods.

$\mathcal{N}eedlewoman$

ELSIE HARMON TRIVETTE

SHE IS IN HER MID-EIGHTIES and plagued with cataractal eyes and arthritic knees. She stays indoors on spring days when her predilection is to work among the flowers, or to look in from time to time on the three robin nestlings that stretch their long necks whenever they hear movement beneath the eaves.

Still, ailments and all, Elsie Harmon Trivette labors every weekday "and most times of a night." Hard work has been the constant of her life; if she could not be productive she would rather die.

Today she shuffles out to the handicap ramp that runs off the porch of her Silverstone Road home. She grins, cane in hand, and declares in an almost inaudible voice, "I see my directions got you here."

Then laboriously she leads the way into the living room. A daughter whom she introduces as Leniavell emerges from another room. "Leniavell stays with me," says Elsie. "And another daughter, June, lives right there across the yard in the white trailer. Then there's another daughter lives down the road. Evanell. I picked odd names."

In her bedroom, just off the parlor, she wants to show examples of her craft. She says people come to the house from everywhere to see her handiwork.

Elsie Harmon Trivette, Zionville, North Carolina

"A woman and a man come here from Des Moines, Iowa. The woman, from a magazine, called and wanted to know about my bedspreads. Wanted to come down here. Said there'd be no pay. I said, 'I don't care,' and they come anyway. Brought eight suitcases, and they's just all around; stayed two days; the man stayed in that room all one day taking pictures of that candlewick bedspread."

She says that, although the woman had told her to expect nothing, there came in the mail within a couple of weeks a check for two hundred dollars.

Elsie runs her hand across the cover of her bed. She says some people call it French knotting and some call it colonial knotting, but others call it candlewick, because wicks are often used for the heavy knotting thread. She does not want to sell the spread and could not set a price on it even if she "was a mind to." A craft specialist at the State Fair at Raleigh once questioned her and then figured she had spent five hundred hours on the cover; that did not include time on the lacework.

Holding up the index finger of her right hand, she shows a bulging callus: "A big knot there; most of it I got pulling needles through that bedspread."

Back in the living room Leniavell has laid out a few of her mother's quilts, among them one called "Grandmother's Flower Garden" and another "The Split Rail Fence." Elsie does not use a sewing machine but stitches by hand—"just like my mother did, and her mother." She learned her skills from the women of her family. "My mother and grandmother raised sheep, and we'd card and spin wool. Made our own clothes—hats, dresses, gloves, socks, everything."

At the mention of wool, Leniavell leaves the room and soon returns with an antique spinning wheel. She adjusts it before her seated mother, who then takes up two rectangular implements, which she explains are for carding wool. Each has angled wire teeth that are closely set on boards of leather. She lays a small handful of wool on one card and begins to comb it with the other. Soon the fibers take the shape of a fluffy dust ball, which is then fed into the spindle. With her foot Elsie activates the large wheel, and the rotating spindle twists the fibers into woolen yarn.

She says people are always curious about spinning wheels.

"Goldie Hawn," she says. "You know this movie star? I taught her how to spin. Yeah, she came here. Her and Kurt Russell both came. That's her husband. He was making a movie on Beech Mountain. And he bought Goldie a spinning wheel. Wanted to find if somebody could teach her how to spin."

Russell brought a spinning wheel to Elsie's house ahead of his wife, whom Elsie had never seen on television.

"Well, then she came over. Nice. Real nice. We just loved her. The nicest people you've ever seen. Just as common as they could be. She stayed all day for two days, and when it was over she could spin good."

From the shelf behind the sofa Elsie takes down a photograph mounted in an antique sterling-silver frame. "Goldie sent the frame, and I put the picture in it—Goldie and her youngun and me'n a granddaughter. That was in the late eighties, I think it was."

As Elsie talks Leniavell brings in other pieces of her mother's work: wall hangings, crocheted afghans, and hook rugs and a robe made from burlap fibers. Several years ago Elsie made a six-foot-by-four-foot rug for a museum in Raleigh, and she received two thousand dollars for it. She shakes her head slowly as she describes how she unraveled the burlap, colored it with vegetable dyes, and hooked the fibers over. "Takes a long time."

"Vegetable dyes?"

"Yes, that's all I use. Natural dyes." She picks up a crocheted afghan that is a blend of earth colors. "I spun this on the wheel, and I dyed it with things like barks, leaves, grass. I use natural dyes for everything. Just get out here and get some things. That yellow there is from onion hulls. The outside is from tomato vines. The brown is walnut. Somewhere in there is dye from beets. I forget what-all I used on this afghan, but that rug there, I remember most of what's in it. I make these dyes from just about anything—lots of times from rusty nails, even kitchen matches. I boil the matches, and they make the prettiest pink. I make dyes from about anything—banana peels, goldenrod, anything."

Because of magazine articles and craft fairs, Elsie's reputation has spread. In her Watauga County home, about a mile from the Tennessee Valley Divide, she welcomes visitors who "just want to find out who I am." Although she thinks most of her traveling days are behind her, she has been to many places to show her mountain skills at spinning, needlework, and even cooking.

"Stayed a week in Sandusky, Ohio. Been to Washington; Cincinnati; Berea, Kentucky; Newport, Rhode Island. Can't think of the places I went to. In Sandusky I stayed five weeks. They put me up in a log cabin. I'd cook beans and bake cornbread." She laughs. "They'd smell the beans and cornbread, and here they'd come. Had to put a rope around the cabin to keep them off. One woman come by and said, 'I smell something that's good.' It was the cornbread. She said, 'Would you give me a piece?' I gave her a piece; couldn't give one to everybody. But she said, 'Oh, honey, I just want one more piece.' Said, 'I never ate nothing like it.' See, she'd never eaten cornbread before."

For twenty-three years Elsie showed her skills at the State Fair in Raleigh. Then in 1994 she was called to accept a Heritage Award.

"Well, we ate at the Governor's Mansion down there, and I could take my family. Leniavell came, and my married daughter Evanell and her husband came. Then that night they had the banquet.

"Everybody [who received an award] had to get up and talk, over a microphone. Well, I told them not to call me until about the middle of the talking. I told them, 'I can't talk.' "

Elsie had never before made a speech, yet she did not want to "break the rules." She arose when the time came and made her way to the stage. She held to the microphone and spoke in a small voice: "It's good to be here. I didn't get a high education, but when you learned something you learned it. I could be dead, but the Lord's blessed me to be so old. I want to thank you for what you've done."

The award hangs in her living room alongside memorabilia such as a large pencil portrait by an admirer from the Midwest.

Elsie's father died when she was two, and the mother reared her brood to be frugal and to work hard. The mother taught the children to farm, to take care of their rambling house, and to do quilting and other needlework.

Elsie never knew why, but the mother did not want the daughters to quilt in the living room.

"We'd go upstairs. We'd take us a pillow and put a hot brick in it. We'd wrap it up in something and put our feet in there, keep them warm. And we'd sit and quilt all day, upstairs in the attic."

When the older children left home Elsie quit the seventh grade. She had never liked classroom work and wanted mightily to stay home and help her mother.

"We lived alone, nobody with us but my brother, and it was hard work. Me'n my mother'd go wash for this woman. Get a dollar for that. One week we'd buy a dollar's worth of flour, and the next week maybe some sugar and coffee."

Elsie gathered more from her mother than the love of needlecraft and chores. She began to do what was normally considered man's work. She learned to be tender-tough, and to have faith against redoubtable odds.

"One morning we got up, and Mama said we's out of flour, so we just had sweet taters and butter. That's all. Then Mama went out to milk for her sister-in-law, and I said, 'Mama, what we gonna do for flour?' Well, she just turned around to me and said, 'The Lord'll make a way.' And I looked up and said, 'Lord, you gonna send flour down here?'

"Later my brother was washing the dishes and I's in the bedroom, and Mama come in just a-laughing. She held out a dollar, and I said, 'You go borrow that?' And Mama said no. Said, 'Aunt Violet gave it to me. She didn't know about the flour, but said she wasn't paying us enough for the washing.' And Mama give me the dollar and said, 'Now you run, get us some flour.' So I went to the store, and ever since then I've just had faith like Mama did. Just had faith; that's what it takes. The Lord provides."

When she was twenty Elsie Harmon married a young man who had grown up in a far hollow of Beech Mountain. Like many others who found the highlands a poor place to make a living, Judson Trivette once left home to seek prosperity. For a few years he worked for a tire maker in Akron, Ohio, but then he returned to be married in his native land.

Where most settlers sought out the valleys and coves to build their homes, Judson and Elsie settled in a small house on a remote knoll a thousand or more feet above Beech Creek. There they farmed and Judson did odd jobs. Then, seven years later, just before their first child was born, Judson "broke down in his nerves" and spent eight months in a hospital. He came home and stayed well for ten years, but from that time until his death in 1983 he was in and out of hospitals and could not help Elsie make her way.

"I had to farm in order to keep the family a-going. I raised tobacco, and I cradled oats, tied them, beat them over a box and got the seed out of them, and saved the seed and got out and sowed more oats; didn't have to spend anything for the cow's feed. I made my own soap out of lye and lard and

cut timber with a crosscut saw; sawed down trees for lumber to fix the house. I took lumber and got me a handsaw. Dug up the old floor, underpinned the house, and floored the porch."

She would hitch a shovel plow to her two little boys, and the three of them would break ground for planting potatoes.

"Oh, but that house was cold. I'd put plastic over the windows, but June and her brothers would stick their fingers through it. We had a coal stove in the living room, and it was not so bad, but in the bedroom it was so cold that I'd lay crossways in the bed with my baby next to me, June next to him, and Reed next to June and Leniavell, all a-trying to keep warm.

"It was so cold in the cow barn that the milk would freeze in the bucket while I was a-milking."

Snow blew under the back door, often causing ice to form across the kitchen floor. At such times the children were gleeful. Breakfast had to wait as they took over the floor and made a skating rink of it. Also in the long winters they played games in the living room. Over the door they attached a hoop made from clothes hangers. Their mother sewed a crude sphere from rags, and with these contrivances the children played basketball.

By the time snow flew in the fall Elsie

and the children had filled their larders. She stored potatoes under a trapdoor. She would kill a hog and take two hams to barter at the store.

"With one ham I'd swap for a hundred pounds of October beans, shell beans; with the other ham I'd buy flour and lard."

Elsie had six children in school at once. She kept a pot of beans on the wood stove; she made kraut from the cabbages of her field; she had corn and potatoes.

She remembers an incident with the beans.

"My youngest son, I guess he was not hardly two. We's eating supper, and he's sitting at the end of the table, just cramming in the beans and paying attention to nobody. All at once it struck me: if I couldn't give him nothing to eat, what would I do? And I jumped up and run out through the kitchen and through the yard. I's a-crying my heart out. And then it came to me: if it come to it I'd go a-begging. Then somebody come running out and said, 'What's the matter?' and I said I didn't know. It was hard on a woman, those harsh times. Six children."

Cash was difficult to come by, but as Leniavell points out, "We were a close family, and we helped each other." So Elsie and the children sold needlecraft and scrounged money in other ways. They gathered and sold clover blooms, wild lettuce, mayapple,

and witch hazel bark. They had their products all ready for pickup when the man came by. Cash from herbs was enough to buy school clothes but little else.

After church one Sunday, Elsie admired the dress of one of the members, and suddenly there appeared a blue sky—or so it seemed.

"I said to her, 'What you been a-doing?' She said, 'Law, I been a-pulling meadow-weed.' Said, 'I bought me a blanket [from the cash] and a new set of silverware. Law, Elsie, I thought you knew about meadow-weed.'

"Well, what she said just excited me to death. And I got home and couldn't wait until Monday morning. I got up and took a half-gallon fruit jar of cornbread and milk. Me'n Leniavell and her brother—they was small—went off down in the woods, and Leniavell went to pulling log moss. We worked down there every day for a solid week. The meadow-weed got on my arms from the elbow down, and it burned bad, but I'd work right on at it. For a solid week I worked; got a big load of meadow-weed.

"My son took the meadow-weed up the road to sell to the man who'd come by. When the man come he asked what the boy had. And my son told him meadow-weed. The man thought for a minute and said, 'I never heard tell of that; never bought nothing like that.'"

Elsie and Leniavell laugh at the practical joke of so long ago.

"Oh, my," says Elsie. "To think we'd been down there in the woods working all day, every day, and wouldn't stop long enough to eat that half-gallon of cornbread and milk. The meadow-weed the woman told me about wasn't worth a dime."

But there were happier incidents.

"I don't know how it happened. Well, like I said, the Lord works things out.

"A catalog came [from the National Bella Hess store], and I had twelve dollars from selling rugs and things. That was after buying schoolbooks. But didn't have enough to get the things Evanell and Leniavell wanted. They wanted the dresses on the front page, for three-ninety-five each. Then June wanted something for a dollar, and the boys wanted something for about two dollars apiece."

Elsie pondered that if she were to get an item for each child, Evanell and Leniavell would have to forgo the three-ninety-five dresses.

"Every now and then those girls would say, 'Mama, we want that dress,' and I'd tell them I just couldn't get it. All I could pay was three dollars. But they wanted that dress *so* bad. It broke my heart, but I ordered the cheaper two-ninety-five dresses."

When at last the parcel came the children gathered around. Elsie hurriedly opened the package, and a note dropped out. The girls' faces fell when their mother read that there were no more of the two-ninety-five dresses. But Elsie read on. Suddenly she threw down the note and rummaged quickly through the box. Leniavell and Evanell held their breath as Elsie pulled out two bright garments—the very dresses they so wanted in the first place. At no extra charge! Also at no additional cost the mail-order people had sent fourteen slips that the Trivettes had not ordered. It was a policy, the note said, to provide items of at least the quality of the goods ordered.

On a spring afternoon Elsie and Leniavell return to the high mountain where they once lived. The small house is no longer habitable; the porch Elsie built has rotted away, and the fields she plowed have been taken over by weeds. Down front on the bank along the crude road are newly sprung creeping flox and irises that Elsie set out more than a half-century ago. Except for a modern house that a son has built a little way down the mountain, all seems the same to Elsie and her daughter.

Across the rim of a great ravine wild cherry trees grow in a stately row. They sway in the wind and frame the peaks far beyond: north to the spine of Beech Mountain's Pinnacle Ridge; west to a range of Tennessee and Virginia mountains that fades into infinity from lush green to misty gray; northeast to the tumble of ridges over which Elsie walked on the tortuous paths and roads to and from Banner Elk.

It is a journey she tried to avoid, but there were times she just had to make it—like the week of Leniavell's infected leg.

"I came home happy; I'd sold a quilt for fifteen dollars. And I found Leniavell on the floor. She was in awful pain, poor little thing, holding her leg. I knew something bad was wrong. Well, I didn't have a way to take her into the Banner Elk hospital. At that time, no horse, not even a mule. So I put her on my hip and walked to the hospital.

"I had to do that, walk all the way in and all the way back—twenty long miles every day for seven days."

She looks out over the wrinkled hills. "We were together then. Hard living but good. Better days than I ever knew."

$\mathcal{F}$olk Champion

ALFRED ADAMS

Glory hallelujah, amen.

I this day, John Adams, being of sound sense and memory, weak of body due to a long complaint, knowing that it is important for a man to die, realizing that my goods might come into the hands of those not deserving, declare this my last will and testament.

I will bequeath my soul to God, who gave it to me, hoping through the merits of a crucified Christ that He will bring both soul and body together in the last day in the mansions of glory.

From his great store of recall, Alfred Adams, in his eighty-eighth year, recites the preamble. "I guess I've read a thousand wills, but this is the only one I've ever seen that began in such a way."

For long years Alfred was Watauga County's banker. Dealing with North Carolina country lawyers, he saw the last will and testament of many a person, but this document—drawn by his great-grandfather John Adams—stands above all others in memory.

The members of Alfred's family always referred to John Adams as "Revolutionary John,"

Alfred Adams, Boone, North Carolina

and they spoke of him offhandedly, as though the old patriarch lived in their time. Alfred cherishes tokens of his forebears; he feels a nearness, as though the long-dead John were a living cousin.

Even now in his old age Alfred is whimsical and fun loving. He entertains guests in a big recreation room and likes to tell old stories. His home rests on a hillock where he can look out over the mountains around Boone—a locale he has never left for long.

It was to the area still called Cove Creek, only a few miles northwest, that Revolutionary John came after the British surrender at Yorktown.

"He was a drummer boy to the troops of the Marquis de Lafayette. [He was] not French or anything like that. Maybe Irish or English. Irish probably, high tempered as we were."

John Adams was among an army of six thousand troops that Lafayette persuaded Louis XVI to send to America. According to a story handed down in the family, when the war ended, John Adams hid in a sugar barrel on a Chesapeake dock as his comrades boarded their sailing ship and headed to France. Soon he learned that soldiers who did not return on the voyage would be charged as deserters.

"Well, that scared him. Don't know why, because everybody was a deserter," says Alfred.

But John Adams took no chances. French warriors had marched to his drumbeat, pursuing Lord Cornwallis across Virginia, and the young man knew the thrill of triumph. Now he wanted to stay in this land of wilderness; he wanted to share its bounty.

First he made his way from Virginia to Philadelphia and there became a craftsman for a cabinet factory. Apparently he also did work on his own.

"We've got contracts yet where he agreed to build something in a workmanlike manner," says Alfred. "There was one where he promised to furnish a slideway toward somebody's house. Slideway, see? It was all woods up in there."

From Philadelphia, Adams sailed to North Carolina. After paddling up the Cape Fear River he continued on foot to Rowan County, where he soon married. Later he trekked westward to the mountains, acquired rich land off Cove Creek, and settled down with his wife, Esther Hawkins Adams, to rear a family and remain for the rest of his life.

The family line from the drummer boy of the 1700s to country banker Alfred Adams is incredibly short. Only three generations separate them.

Revolutionary John's youngest son—an earlier Alfred—was getting up in years when he fathered Tarleton Pulaski Adams, called "Doc." Doc in turn was nearly seventy when he sired today's Alfred Adams by his young wife. Alfred the banker is thus the youngest son of the youngest son of the youngest son of Lafayette's drummer boy.

An oddity within an oddity is that Doc, the father of today's Alfred Adams, was a prisoner during the Civil War. So divisive was that conflict in these parts that although Doc fought for the South his half-brother joined the Union forces. A full brother was killed fighting for the Confederacy.

Doc was at nearby Camp Mast on Cove Creek when Northern soldiers hemmed in his battalion. The encircled Confederates debated a full day and night as to whether they should surrender or fight it out

Says Alfred, "The young bucks would vote to fight, but the old ones wanted to give in. The next morning they put up the white flag, and the Yankees started off with their captives. Over yonder somewhere they stopped. The ones that voted to surrender, they turned loose and let them go home. The others, they took to Ohio. Camp Chase. There Doc Adams spent the rest of the war."

After the Confederate surrender at Appomattox, Union officials at Camp Chase would muster the prisoners each morning. Those who took the oath of allegiance would be free to go home. But Doc Adams's mulish ways kept him there.

"Every morning they let a few go. But my daddy was too stubborn to take the oath. Then one morning he went around behind the formation. Still not taking the oath, he rolled his blanket and just walked out with the men who did."

It was spring, and Doc Adams was sick with fever. He and his comrades were eager to get home to put out a crop. He left on the third of March, and Alfred's aunt—Doc's sister—remembers that he arrived at Cove Creek in June.

"Walked all the way," says Alfred. "It was cold that month. And when he came to a river I reckon he just took off his clothes and held them over his head and walked on. Don't know how the other fellows waited for him; he was pretty weak."

Doc's farm prospered. He worked the crops in the warm months and taught himself Latin in the long winters. He also went to school in the county courthouse in Boone. In 1868 he was authorized to teach. Professor Henry Dixon, who came up from Alamance after the war, inscribed on Doc Adams's certificate that "his work was satisfactory, he conducted himself as becomes a gentlemen, and I pronounce him capable of teaching in all branches of our common schools." When he entered his profession Tarleton Pulaski Adams became more commonly known by his initials, T. P.

For forty-four years Adams was the head of Watauga County's school board. John Preston Arthur, in his *History of Watauga County*, wrote that in 1905 Adams traveled at his own expense to Raleigh to urge support for a new training school. Alfred remembers that his father made the trip many times.

In the late fall of that same year, when a local school building was left exposed to the Appalachian elements, Adams carried mortar and brick. He kept at it for a month, stopping only after a roof was put into place.

It is fitting that he would lead the development of Silverstone School near his homeplace, a facility that became known as the best in the high mountains.

Alfred Adams, though long retired, goes often to an office provided by a successor bank. He has seen slow but resolute change in the mountains, and he thinks some people want to cling to the past more than others. He respects the differences—whether people want to live in yesterday or tomorrow.

"Now the old-timers all had a code that they lived by. And you didn't infringe on that code; you didn't change it. Their word was what they lived by. If they told you and shook hands with you, that was it. Oh, there were a few liars around, but everybody knew who they were. Most people just went on your word."

As a banker Alfred knew well the importance of capital in running farms and businesses. Intimacy with the region assured him a long career. Like his father he wanted the mountain people to be educated. He also wanted roads, buildings, industry. He sought better lives for his people, but within such progress he wanted to preserve the mountains' customs and beauty.

"After I got into the bank Demps Wilcox and Glenn Andrews and me'n a bunch of us got to getting some industry in here. We'd just find us a prospect, and we'd form an eleemosynary corporation and put up a building. The bank would carry it for a little under market, and that usually helped us construct it. Then the bank was repaid for the rent. Profits went to either the hospital or the college. That's the way we got industry into Boone."

With every new factory, however, the terrain is altered. New sources of money mean new homes. Shops and complexes spring up in and around the urban areas. One highway that did not even exist forty years ago is now populated over its entire twenty-five-mile length.

"When we were rebuilding a road from here to Blowing Rock," says Alfred, "the ecologists and environmentalists got wind of it and tried to block the effort. We were having a hearing before the highway commission, and they asked me if I'd make a statement.

"I said, 'Gentlemen, I lived up here when the ecology and the environment was all that was here.'"

Industry and change are loathed by those who want to keep the mountains pure. But there have been visionaries such as the late Dougherty brothers, D. D. and B. B., who believed the beauty of the mountains and the progress of the people could coexist. They led the fight early in the century to found a college in Boone, and Alfred's father helped them. All doggedly battled for education and industry. All felt that advancement would one day change the mountain life they once knew. Yet even as the flat valley of Daniel Boone Creek yields to steel and concrete, Alfred is convinced that proper planning and zoning can provide commercial gain while protecting the mountain world he loves.

"I didn't even know mountain people were poor till I got grown. Never wanted to get away from Watauga; a lot of my family didn't. I doubt if old Enoch Adams was out of the county three times in his life. Cousin of mine. Dead now. These folks just liked to stay around home."

But most young men fanned out to places like Cincinnati and Detroit, where they could earn a better living. Alfred remembers that when he finished high school at Cove Creek all but two of his eighteen male classmates left the county to find work.

"There was nothing here. Nothing. There was no payroll. The college worked a few people, and there were a few peckerwood sawmills around—ten hours a day, fifteen and twenty cents an hour—but there just wasn't anything to do."

Big colleges were too expensive, but Alfred's widowed mother wanted for her son the advantages her husband might have provided. Alfred would indeed go to school, to a small college in the mountains; the mother would take her children; they would go along to help him. At Mars Hill College, not far from Asheville, the family worked until Alfred graduated.

After becoming a banker Alfred decided

his new work was "probably better than being a mechanic." As a boy he had pictured himself creating, repairing, and tinkering with things. But he found that in the bank he could do things for people much as his father had; he could make their lives better, bring opportunities. This was the lodestone that drew him from wrenches and pulleys and propelled him toward a stronger challenge.

Lending money so hardworking people could open a business appealed to him. He remembered neighbors who had talent but never the means for putting it to proper use.

Over the years he lent millions in seed capital, but as he looks back over his career he finds the small accommodations stick in his mind equally with the big ones.

"I let two boys—one nine and the other fourteen—let them have six hundred and fifty dollars to put in an acre of strawberries. Nobody on the note but the two boys, wasn't even a legal note. And the first year the boys sold thirty-six hundred dollars' worth.

"I lent a little twelve-year-old girl twenty dollars to put down a bed of strawberries. Didn't charge her any interest. She'd just pick strawberries and would pay me back, you know.

"Kids used to go down in the Piedmont and buy a heifer calf off of these dairymen, three- or four-day-old calves for thirty dollars. I lent them the money, and they'd grow out the calf and sell it back in a couple of years to one of the same dairymen. Sell it for maybe four hundred when it grew to the milk-producing age.

"Must have been a thousand people told me that I loaned them the first money they ever borrowed."

There are those he started off with as little as a thousand dollars who are now millionaires.

"One fellow came in one day and said, 'Alfred, I want to bring you a fat hen.' I told him there was no reason to do that. He said, 'Well, the first money you loaned to me, I didn't have a thing in the world.' He said, 'Now I've got many, many acres. They're paid for, the house is paid for, and I've got all those chicken houses, and I grow all those chickens.' He told me how much a year he made, because of that first loan.

"That kind of satisfaction probably beats mechanicking."

In his youth Alfred's passion was working with tools; his calling was to make the most of his native skills. Although he was to become a banker to thousands of mountain people, his intrigue for mechanical things remains. Today in his backyard he has a blacksmith shop. He sometimes rebuilds old cars.

Alfred recalls when there were no asphalt roads in the county and people traveled in either mud or dust, according to the weather. In winter the roads could be impossible to travel. If there was an impasse people would take out a roadside fence and bypass through a farmer's field.

Such was the feeling the poor had for the other poor. They were selfless in the way of Tarleton Pulaski Adams; they were generous in the way of his son Alfred the banker, who lent money from his own pocket for a little girl to buy strawberries.

ADAMS ANECDOTES: A SAMPLER

On a good friend's politics:

"My old friend up the road is what we call a 'professional mountaineer.' Now he can spot a tourist a mile off. He dances a little, but he's getting old now.

"They got him to be judge in an election once. After a while they could tell he wasn't enjoying it much, but he stuck with it. About ten o'clock that evening the votes were getting counted out, and there was just a handful of people still there. And my friend says, 'Fellers, ain't this just about over?' And they said it was. And he asked them if there was anybody there who'd mind if he made a little speech. They said that would be all right, and he got up on the table and said, 'Fellers, this ain't like it ought to be. Here's Democrats watching Republicans, Republicans watching Democrats, and neighbors watching neighbors. And that ought not to be. I'll have you to know that I love ever' one of ye, and I fairly enjoyed today. But it'll be a cold day in hell that any of you ever get me back in here.' "

On Will and the bucking bull:

"There was a Tennessee family, noted horse people, who staged rodeos back in the twenties. The idea seemed profitable, so a group in Boone decided to have a rodeo. They put a saddle on a bull and persuaded old Will, a popular character in town, to ride it.

"Well, old Will had been drinking a good bit, but they got him on the bull, and the bull started bucking. The saddle started turning, and old Will was hanging on to the saddle horn, and the sponsors saw there would be trouble, so they got hold of the bull and quieted it down. Old Will got down from the bull and dusted himself off. The sponsors asked if Will was hurt.

" 'No,' he said, 'I ain't hurt. But the damn show's over.' "

Luthier and Picker

WAYNE HENDERSON

EONS AGO, off the slopes of Virginia's highest mountain, a great river—now a narrow, rushing stream called the Big Wilson—carved out a broad, verdant valley. Today in that valley, just beyond the sound of the Big Wilson's tumbling waters, lies a hamlet called Rugby, a place rarely recognized on any map. Within Rugby's loosely defined boundaries are several structures—a store, a real-estate office, and a rescue-squad building. In a converted country store by the road is a luthier's workshop. It is here that Wayne Henderson makes guitars and mandolins and, more rarely, banjos, violins, and dulcimers.

Wayne has lived in the valley all his life. Though his guitars and mandolins are in demand around the globe, and though he has played his guitar for audiences from Sri Lanka to Africa to Europe, his adamant choice is never to leave Rugby for long; though he often travels to far-off lands he remains a Virginia mountaineer, never expecting to be anything else.

From the high mountain three large, white barns with mansard roofs are visible a mile or so west of the workshop. Nestled among the barns is a two-story brick home, the center of hundreds of acres of farmland that Breece and Kate Tucker once owned. They were the most prosperous of the gentle people living in Big Wilson Valley.

As a boy Wayne often did light work on the Tuckers' sprawling farm. In pretty weather he would walk home from the two-room school up the road from the farm. On the way he enjoyed the beauty of Breece and Kate's land, and it floated in his boy's mind that one day, when the couple had grown too old for the farm, perhaps he could live in the brick house. He never told a living soul. The fantasy was one to enjoy but not really believe.

Today Breece and Kate are long dead, and their brick home and vast farm have been sold two or three times over. A few years ago, when the owner decided to sell the dwelling, he offered it to Wayne, who had once told him he loved the place. At last a boy's dream became real, as Wayne—now in his mid-forties and frugally successful—moved into the old Tucker homeplace.

His parents' farm almost touched the Tucker spread; the Henderson place lay off a narrow, winding highway just around the bend and to the south. Like everyone else in the valley Wayne came from a family that tinkered in crafts and enjoyed the spirited but often lonely music that originated in old Scotland, Ireland, and England. His father, a dawn-to-dusk farmer and the son of a blacksmith, was a Saturday-night fiddler with the Rugby Gullyjumpers,

Wayne Henderson, Rugby, Virginia

who played at country dances on nearby York Ridge and in homes where the hosts rolled back rugs and asked neighbors in for jamborees.

Wayne cannot remember when his passion for mountain music dawned, but at age five he began to play his brother's Montgomery Ward guitar. His hands were so small that he could not reach around the instrument's neck, so he made sweet sounds by laying the old Recording King guitar in his lap, pressing the strings with his thumb, and strumming with the other hand. By the age of eight his hands had grown so that he could at last reach around the fret board to form the chords.

Wayne's father almost never practiced his music. His fiddle lay in a drawer until those nights when he pulled it out, tuned it, and took it to perform with the Gullyjumpers. Now he wanted to support his young son's interest. Whenever his work—laboring in the tobacco fields and tending cattle—was done, he would tune his fiddle, and son Wayne would strum the rhythm. In the parlor they played Carter Family songs like "Wildwood Flower" and "Jimmy Brown" and fiddle tunes like "Arkansas Traveler" and "Ragtime Annie." It was during these times that Wayne thought his father was happiest.

The boy's passion for the guitar grew strong. On Saturday nights his grandparents would listen to the Grand Ole Opry, and little Wayne would come over and sit for hours with them as they huddled around the only radio in the valley strong enough to bring in the Nashville signal. While they listened they shelled corn they would later feed to the chickens. Into the early-morning hours they listened to the Opry.

The grandparents were fondest of the singing and picking of Uncle Dave Macon and the harmonica playing of DeFord Bailey. Wayne favored the finger style of Sam McGee, an aging guitarist who always performed just after midnight. During the following week, after hearing his hero play, Wayne would take down his brother's guitar and imitate McGee. He wanted mightily to see the old man perform one day.

While the sound of his brother's guitar was acceptable, its neck was too large. Also the instrument was not his own. The desire to have his own guitar started Wayne on the road to becoming an admired luthier and performer.

He would watch and listen as local legend E. C. Ball played a Martin guitar—"the best guitar made," says Wayne—at Ball's small store down the road.

"He was real particular with that nice old Martin," remembers Wayne. It was "his most prized possession. He bought it for a hundred dollars—a lot of money in this neck of the woods. He'd bring that Martin to the store on days when he didn't have much business. He'd play, and I'd go in there and listen. He'd show me some chords and licks, and I'd watch him. Couldn't understand how in the world a guitar could sound so good as that one did."

It was just this kind of guitar—a "nice old Martin"—that Wayne wanted to own. He began thinking, "That good Martin was made just out of wood, and I ought to be able to make one." He had learned much by watching one grandfather repair watches and the other carve wood. He himself had whittled chain links, slingshots, and little boxes with balls in them. Why then could he not make a guitar?

He studied Ball's guitar and noted carefully its pattern and construction. Bending good wood for the guitar's body would be difficult.

Months later he discovered by accident that heavy walnut veneer covered the bottom of his mother's dresser drawer. Stealthily he slipped out the bottom piece and placed it in the creek, letting water run over it to loosen the veneer. The next day he carefully bent the veneer into the shape of a guitar box. Through the summer he worked to fashion the guitar's body and the head, neck, fret board, and bridge. Having no glue, he borrowed his father's black rubber adhesive, but when he assembled the pieces and dried them outdoors the sun melted the rubber and the black goo ran over the crafted wood. His summer's work was destroyed.

The father sensed Wayne's anguish. In his old pickup truck he took the boy to visit Albert Hash, an extraordinary craftsman who was working in a shop just over the North Carolina border. Hash had made his own first fiddle; instantly he understood the boy's disappointment.

"He got out a fiddle he had made," remembers Wayne. "I thought it was absolutely the most beautiful thing I'd even seen, made out of curly wood from an old bedstead, carvings and inlays all over it. I could not figure out how anybody could make an instrument like that."

Hash fished around and came up with part of an old door made of Philippine mahogany. He gave Wayne a piece large enough to draw a pattern upon and told the boy how to shape a guitar body by soaking the wood in water and bending it over a hot pipe. He told of someone he knew who was refinishing a Martin guitar with the strings removed—a perfect model for Wayne to inspect. Without the taut wires in place to maintain tension, the inside of the guitar could be inspected; the boy could look into the sound hole and see how the body was constructed. Perhaps this would allow him to discover the secrets of a Martin guitar's throaty tone.

Back home, laying the mahogany on the kitchen table, Wayne drew a basic pattern for a guitar. All summer he worked not to make a cheap instrument but to fashion a fine one—one that would cause Albert Hash to grin and pat him on the back.

Using only his pocketknife Wayne carved blocks of intricate inlay from small wood pieces, then set them around the edge of the guitar. From slivers of a cow's bone he spent days filing six bridge pins. Today even for the finest guitars such pins are plastic and sell for less than a dollar a set.

"The first thing I wanted to do was take that guitar to Mr. Hash," says Wayne. "I was so proud of it, and it played pretty good, better than the old guitar I'd played. And Albert bragged on it something awful. Said, 'Why, son, you've absolutely outdone yourself here.' Said, 'I could not believe you could make a guitar out of this old piece of wood.' Said, 'I should have given you better wood.' He just made me feel like I'd done something really big."

From his catalogs Albert Hash ordered enough rosewood for Wayne to build a second guitar. Meanwhile the young man studied the makings of fine instruments. He learned that abalone was used for the inlay of Martin guitars, and he used that shell to embellish his next two instruments; he sold these for enough money to buy quality materials and tools.

After his sixth or seventh guitar—he doesn't remember which—a thing happened that told him his future might not be in farming, but perhaps in making guitars.

"After my grandfather passed away I'd go stay with my grandmother of a night. And I made another guitar and did all the abalone inlay, cutting out all the pieces with a file, because I didn't have a jeweler's saw. The guitar I made was right pretty. It sounded good."

One late afternoon a frightening thing happened. He and his grandmother watched with open mouths as the local moonshiner drove up, bringing with him a stranger.

"Me being a youngster, I was scared of him. My folks talked about him, said, 'Oh, he's got a still. Don't want to be around that man.'

"I thought, 'This stranger, if he knows the moonshiner, he's bound to be a crook himself,' and I was afraid of him. Kept my eye on him."

The two men came in, and the unsmiling stranger began, "I heard you made a guitar."

Wayne showed him the instrument, and the man took it, sat down, and began to play. Then he looked up and smiled.

"He had fits about it," says Wayne. "Said, 'I believe this is the best-sounding guitar I've ever played.' Wanted to know if I'd sell it."

Wayne demurred. Besides having a fondness for the instrument he remained skeptical of the man: "I was afraid of him, afraid he'd try to steal my guitar."

Wayne kept repeating that he did not want to sell the guitar, but the stranger persisted: "You'd sell it for a price, wouldn't you?"

Again Wayne shook his head. Then, hoping to end the session, he suddenly said he would take five hundred dollars, a price he knew to be astronomical for the times. The stranger kept playing, then finally stopped and handed the guitar to Wayne, indicating to his bootlegger friend that he was ready to depart.

"I was relieved. I told my granny that I made the price unreal so the stranger wouldn't hang around."

The next afternoon at his grandmother's he looked out and saw the stranger approaching alone. The man knocked and asked to play the guitar again. After a half-hour Wayne and his grandmother began to worry. Then the stranger stopped playing and arose from his chair. From his shirt pocket he pulled a wad of bills. "I think I'm just going to take this guitar," he said as he handed five hundred-dollar bills to Wayne. It was more money than the boy had ever seen.

"So I told my granny, 'If I can make money like this for guitars, that's what I'm going to do.'"

From the proceeds Wayne bought more tools. Neighbors told others about his gift and industry. He began repairing musical instruments for people from Rugby, Volney, Damascus, and throughout the area of Mount Rogers and Whitetop Mountain. From a smashed Martin guitar that was brought to him he learned "every angle and every piece" of what he considered the finest brand ever made.

And the business began coming in. "I've been totally behind ever since," he says.

For two reasons, he decided to become a rural mail carrier. First, the job would provide insurance and retirement benefits. Second, it would vary his day so he would not be totally confined to the shop.

His reputation spread. He visited the shops of the Martin and Gibson guitar companies and discovered that the difference between his work and theirs was that they had separate specialists making each piece of a guitar; Wayne made all his guitar's parts, and he alone assembled the instrument.

In Nashville, George Gruhn heard about Wayne. Gruhn's firm repaired guitars for the rich and famous of the music world—Elvis Presley, Kris Kristofferson, and Johnny Cash among them. He asked Wayne to join his shop, but Wayne did not want to leave Rugby for long.

Nonetheless, to help Randy Wood—"one of my favorite craftspeople, a man covered up with work"—Wayne tore himself away from Rugby for a few weeks at a time. He stayed in Nashville with a cousin and worked many long hours with Wood.

It was on one of these occasions that George Gruhn paved the way for what would become Wayne's biggest thrill. He introduced the young man to a guard at the Grand Ole Opry, which stood near Gruhn's shop. Soon Wayne enjoyed the guard's confidence. On Wayne's occasional visits his new friend allowed him to go backstage. There he at last met his idol—Sam McGee, the guitar picker of the midnight Saturdays when Wayne had listened by the radio with his grandparents in faraway Rugby. As the months passed the two became friends.

"There's nobody in the world that I could get a bigger thrill out of sitting down and talking to. He was just a wonderful person, like your grandpaw. He was in his eighties, but he could still play pretty good.

"I think he liked me up there. I'd take him a guitar and show him. He was interested in guitars, especially in some young kid that tried to play like he did. He would show me licks on the guitar.

"I even got to sit down and pick with him. Every time I would go in there he'd say, 'I'll show you how to do this,' and I was in hog heaven, sitting there and picking with Sam McGee, somebody I used to sit up until after midnight just to hear on the radio."

One Saturday night as the two were playing a tune backstage, a stagehand came and told McGee that he was soon to go on the air.

"Why don't you just go play this tune with me?" McGee asked his young companion.

"Lord have mercy," says Wayne, thinking back to the time. "I was in my old, dusty jeans and not really dressed good, and the Grand Ole Opry was the most famous show in the world."

To his own surprise Wayne turned down the chance to play rhythm for the noted Sam McGee. Besides not being prepared to go on, the thought ran through his mind that McGee might get into trouble by bringing a nonunion performer onto the stage.

Wayne now regards that quick decision as his life's greatest blunder.

A thing happened soon after that would prevent any hope of redeeming the error. His guitarist friend, age eighty-three, died when his farm tractor turned over. At the time Sam McGee was the oldest member of the Grand Ole Opry.

"It would have been worth it [joining McGee onstage] if they had put me in jail. I could then tell people I'd played a tune on the Grand Ole Opry."

Still, greatness in the country-music world has not passed Wayne Henderson by. Not yet fifty years old, he has played in Carnegie Hall, at Wolftrap, and on National

Public Radio. He has made 174 guitars, sixty mandolins, fifteen banjos, two fiddles, and two dulcimers. Henderson instruments are now played in France, Japan, Canada, Mexico—countries around the world.

In 1995 Wayne was made a National Heritage Fellow at a ceremony at the White House, where he met Hillary Clinton. For the event Wayne went out and bought a tie. "Didn't even know how to tie it," he says. "But I had to get spruced up—going to the White House."

It was there that he met fellow mountaineer Bea Hensley, another award winner. "I really liked hanging out with him," says Wayne. "The people on my daddy's side were blacksmiths, but not like Bea. He's an artist. The stuff he does just totally amazes me."

Wayne found he could best talk with people like Bea and cowboy poet Buck Ramsey. Also there was his friend Joe Wilson, a member of the National Council for Traditional Arts, who once lived in Mountain City, ninety minutes away from Rugby, in East Tennessee.

In his travels over the world—to places like Pakistan, Thailand, Canada, Indonesia, Hong Kong, the Philippines, Korea, Africa, Oman, and Bahrain—Wayne has discovered the universality of music.

He marvels at how the people of Sri Lanka, "hid back among the mountains," could enjoy the Americans' performances.

"We played some old-timey fiddle tunes, and pianist Jeff Little [who grew up not far from Wayne] played B. B. King blues. To start with we'd get polite applause, but by the end of the show they'd be pretty much excited. They were clapping and whistling and hollering. Got into it. I'm sure they had not been used to that kind of music."

Most of Wayne's travel has been sponsored by the United States Information Agency. The experience has provided him with insights not possible through geography books and television. He has seen beauty, yes, but nothing so placid or spectacular as the mountain land around Rugby.

He has also seen despair far uglier than anything he ever imagined back in the valley. In Karachi armored cars transported him, and guards with submachine guns paraded before his hotel; he saw citizens with automatic weapons standing by their gardens. In other places the pollution was so bad that traffic police wore masks.

Wayne looks out a window of his Tucker Road house. From the northwest windows he can see the white building, now a neighbor's dwelling, that was once the two-room school he attended. Across the road a stand of cultivated Fraser firs runs high on the hillside toward the old schoolhouse. To the south cattle graze around a caretaker's old place.

The Gruhn firm long ago offered Wayne a job that would have paid more than he earned making guitars. Also a band from Nashville asked him to join it as a guitarist to play permanently on the Grand Ole Opry.

He refused these opportunities. He intends to stay put in his comfortable Rugby, a place he has found without equal in all his travels. In an environment that many a resort developer would admire, Rugby continues to be rural in every way. Though several outsiders have moved in, the valley and village absorb them without surrendering tranquility or beauty.

The monuments of Wayne Henderson's past remain. And friends in Big Wilson Valley say he is unaffected by his mountain-music fame.

Index

Wood, Randy, 121
Woody, Artur, 24, 29
Woody, Claude, 22–23, 25–27
Woody, Martin, 22, 23, 24, 28, 29
Woody, Max, 21–30

Yadkin River, 54
Yancey County Institute, 46
Yellowhammer Gap, 52

Zionhill, 31, 32, 35. *See also* Windy Gap
Zionville, 100